The Doré Bible Gallery

GUSTAVE DORÉ.

THE

DORÉ BIBLE GALLERY,

CONTAINING

ONE HUNDRED SUPERB ILLUSTRATIONS, AND A PAGE OF EXPLANATORY LETTER-PRESS FACING EACH.

ILLUSTRATED BY

GUSTAVE DORÉ.

CHICAGO:
MORRILL, HIGGINS & CO.
1892.

W. B. CONKEY CO.
PRINTERS AND BINDERS
CHICAGO

PREFACE.

This volume, as its title indicates, is a collection of engravings illustrative of the Bible—the designs being all from the pencil of the greatest of modern delineators, Gustave Doré The original work, from which this collection has been made, met with an immediate and warm recognition and acceptance among those whose means admitted of its purchase, and its popularity has in no wise diminished since its first publication, but has even extended to those who could only enjoy it casually, or in fragmentary parts That work, however, in its entirety, was far too costly for the larger and ever-widening circle of M Doré's admirers and to meet the felt and often-expressed want of this class, and to provide a volume of choice and valuable designs upon sacred subjects for art-loving Biblical students generally, this work was projected and has been carried forward The aim has been to introduce subjects of general interest—that is, those relating to the most prominent events and personages of Scripture—those most familiar to all readers, the plates being chosen with special reference to the known taste of the American people To each cut is prefixed a page of letter-press, in narrative form, and containing generally a brief analysis of the design Aside from the labors of the editor and publishers, the work, while in progress, was under the pains-taking and careful scrutiny of artists and scholars not directly interested in the undertaking, but still having a generous solicitude for its success It is hoped, therefore, that its general plan and execution will render it acceptable both to the appreciative and friendly patrons of the great artist, and to those who would wish to possess such a work solely as a choice collection of illustrations upon sacred themes.

GUSTAVE DORÉ.

The subject of this sketch is, perhaps, the most original and variously gifted designer the world has ever known. At an age when most men have scarcely passed their novitiate in art, and are still under the direction and discipline of their masters and the schools, he had won a brilliant reputation, and readers and scholars everywhere were gazing on his work with ever-increasing wonder and delight at his fine fancy and multifarious gifts. He has raised illustrative art to a dignity and importance before unknown, and has developed capacities for the pencil before unsuspected. He has laid all subjects tribute to his genius, explored and embellished fields hitherto lying waste, and opened new and shining paths and vistas where none before had trod To the works of the great he has added the lustre of his genius, bringing their beauties into clearer view and warming them to a fuller life

His delineations of character, in the different phases of life from the horrible to the grotesque, the grand to the comic, attest the versatility of his powers, and, whatever faults may be found by critics, the public will heartily render their quota of admiration to his magic touch, his rich and facile rendering of almost every thought that stirs, or lies yet dormant, in the human heart It is useless to attempt a sketch of his various beauties, those who would know them best must seek them in the treasure-house that his genius is constantly augmenting with fresh gems and wealth To one, however, of his most prominent traits we will refer—his wonderful rendering of the powers of Nature

His early wanderings in the wild and romantic passes of the Vosges doubtless developed this inherent tendency of his mind. There he wandered, and there, mayhap, imbibed that deep delight of wood and valley, mountain-pass and rich ravine, whose variety of form and detail seems endless to the enchanted eye He has caught the very spell of the wilderness, she has laid her hand upon him, and he has gone forth with her blessing So bold and truthful and minute are his countless representations of forest scenery, so delicate the tracery of branch and stem, so patriarchal the giant boles of his woodland monarchs, that the gazer is at once satisfied and entranced His vistas lie slumbering with repose either in shadowy glade or fell ravine, either with glint of lake or the glad, long course of some rejoicing stream, and above all, supreme in a beauty all its own, he spreads a canopy of peerless sky, or a wilderness, perhaps, of angry storm, or peaceful stretches of soft, fleecy cloud, or heavens serene and fair—another kingdom to his teeming art, after the earth has rendered all her gifts.

Paul Gustave Doré was born in the city of Strasburg, January 10, 1833 Of his boyhood we have no very particular account At eleven years of age, however, he essayed his first artistic creation—a set of lithographs, published in his native city The following year found him in Paris, entered as a student at the Charlemagne Lyceum His first actual work began in 1848, when his fine series of sketches, the "Labors of Hercules," was given to the public through the medium of an illustrated journal with which he was for a long time connected as designer In 1856 were published the illustrations for Balzac's "Contes Drolatiques" and those for "The Wandering Jew"—the first humorous and grotesque in the highest degree—indeed, showing a perfect abandonment to fancy, the other weird and supernatural, with fierce battles, shipwrecks, turbulent mobs, and nature in her most forbidding and terrible aspects Every incident or suggestion that could possibly make the story more effective, or add to the horror of the scenes was seized upon and portrayed with wonderful power These at once gave the young designer a great reputation, which was still more enhanced by his subsequent works

With all his love for nature and his power of interpreting her in her varying moods, Doré was a dreamer, and many of his finest achievements were in the realm of the imagination But he was at home in the actual world also, as witness his designs for "Atala," "London—a Pilgrimage," and many of the scenes in "Don Quixote"

When account is taken of the variety of his designs, and the fact considered that in almost every task he attempted none had ventured before him, the amount of work he accomplished is fairly incredible To enumerate the immense tasks he undertook—some single volumes alone containing hundreds of illustrations—will give some faint idea of his industry Besides those already mentioned are Montaigne, Dante, the Bible, Milton, Rabelais, Tennyson's "Idyls of the King," "The Ancient Mariner," Shakespeare, "Legende de Croquemitaine," "La Fontaine's Fables," and others still

Take one of these works—the Dante, La Fontaine, or, "Don Quixote"—and glance at the pictures. The mere hand labor involved in their production is surprising; but when the quality of the work is properly estimated, what he accomplished seems prodigious No particular mention need be made of him as painter or sculptor, for his reputation rests solely upon his work as an illustrator.

Doré's nature was exuberant and buoyant, and he was youthful in appearance He had a passion for music, possessed rare skill as a violinist, and it is assumed that, had he failed to succeed with his pencil, he could have won a brilliant reputation as a musician

He was a bachelor, and lived a quiet, retired life with his mother—married, as he expressed it to her and his art His death occurred on January 23, 1883.

LIST OF ILLUSTRATIONS.

THE CREATION OF EVE

"And the Lord God said, it is not good that the man should be alone, I will make him a helpmeet for him . And the Lord God caused a deep sleep to fall on Adam, and he slept, and he took one of his ribs, and closed up the flesh instead thereof, and the rib which the Lord God had taken from man, made he a woman, and brought her unto the man And Adam said, This is now bone of my bone and flesh of my flesh she shall be called Woman, because she was taken out of man Therefore shall a man leave his father and mother, and shall cleave unto his wife, and they shall be one flesh"—*Genesis ii, 18, 21-24*

In these few words the Scriptures narrate the creation of the first mother of our race In "Paradise Lost," the poetic genius of Milton, going more into detail describes how Eve awoke to consciousness, and found herself reposing under a shade of flowers, much wondering what she was and whence she came Wandering by the margin of a small lake, she sees her own form mirrored in the clear waters, at which she wonders more But a voice is heard, leading her to him for whom she was made, who lies sleeping under a grateful shade It is at this point the artist comes to interpret the poet's dream Amid the varied and luxurious foliage of Eden, in the vague light of the early dawn, Eve is presented, coy and graceful, gazing on her sleeping Lord, while in the background is faintly outlined the mystic form of Him in whose image they were created

G. Doré

THE EXPULSION FROM THE GARDEN.

And the Lord God said, Behold, the man is become as one of us, to know good and evil; and now, lest he put forth his hand, and take also of the tree of life, and eat, and live forever: Therefore, the Lord God sent him forth from the garden of Eden, to till the ground from whence he was taken. So he drove out the man; and he placed at the east of the garden of Eden cherubims, and a flaming sword which turned every way, to keep the way of the tree of life.—*Genesis iii, 22–24.*

They, looking back, all the eastern side beheld
Of Paradise, so late their happy seat,
Waved over by that flaming brand; the gate,
With dreadful forces thronged, and fiery arms:
Some natural tears they dropped, but wiped them soon;
The world was all before them, where to choose
Their place of rest, and Providence their guide;
They, hand in hand, with wandering steps and slow,
Through Eden took their solitary way.

Paradise Lost, Book XII.

THE MURDER OF ABEL.

And Adam knew Eve his wife; and she conceived, and bare Cain, and said, I have gotten a man from the Lord. And she again bare his brother Abel. And Abel was a keeper of sheep, but Cain was a tiller of the ground. And in process of time it came to pass, that Cain brought of the fruit of the ground an offering unto the Lord. And Abel, he also brought of the firstlings of his flock and of the fat thereof. And the Lord had respect unto Abel and to his offering: But unto Cain and to his offering he had not respect. And Cain was very wroth, and his countenance fell. And the Lord said unto Cain, Why art thou wroth? and why is thy countenance fallen? If thou doest well, shalt thou not be accepted? and if thou doest not well, sin lieth at the door, and unto thee shall be his desire, and thou shalt rule over him. And Cain talked with Abel his brother: and it came to pass, when they were in the field, that Cain rose up against Abel his brother, and slew him.

And the Lord said unto Cain, Where is Abel thy brother? And he said, I know not: Am I my brother's keeper? And he said, What hast thou done? the voice of thy brother's blood crieth unto me from the ground. And now art thou cursed from the earth, which hath opened her mouth to receive thy brother's blood from thy hand; When thou tillest the ground, it shall not henceforth yield unto thee her strength; a fugitive and a vagabond shalt thou be in the earth. And Cain said unto the Lord, My punishment is greater than I can bear. Behold, thou hast driven me out this day from the face of the earth; and from thy face shall I be hid; and I shall be a fugitive and a vagabond in the earth; and it shall come to pass, that every one that findeth me shall slay me. And the Lord said unto him, Therefore whosoever slayeth Cain, vengeance shall be taken on him sevenfold. And the Lord set a mark upon Cain, lest any finding him should kill him.

And Cain went out from the presence of the Lord, and dwelt in the land of Nod, on the east of Eden.—*Genesis iv, 1–16*

G. Doré

THE DELUGE.

In the six hundredth year of Noah's life, in the second month, the seventeenth day of the month, the same day were all the fountains of the great deep broken up, and the windows of heaven were opened. And the rain was upon the earth forty days and forty nights.

In the selfsame day entered Noah, and Shem, and Ham, and Japheth, the sons of Noah, and Noah's wife, and the three wives of his sons with them, into the ark; they, and every beast after his kind, and all the cattle after their kind, and every creeping thing that creepeth upon the earth after his kind, and every fowl after his kind, every bird of every sort. And they went in unto Noah into the ark, two and two of all flesh, wherein is the breath of life. And they that went in, went in male and female of all flesh, as God had commanded him: and the Lord shut him in.

And the flood was forty days upon the earth; and the waters increased, and bare up the ark, and it was lift up above the earth. And the waters prevailed, and were increased, greatly upon the earth; and the ark went upon the face of the waters. And the waters prevailed exceedingly upon the earth; and all the high hills, that were under the whole heaven, were covered. Fifteen cubits upward did the waters prevail; and the mountains were covered. And all flesh died that moved upon the earth, both of fowl, and of cattle, and of beast, and of every creeping thing that creepeth upon the earth, and every man; all in whose nostrils was the breath of life, of all that was in the dry land, died. And every living substance was destroyed which was upon the face of the ground, both man and cattle, and the creeping things, and the fowl of the heaven; and they were destroyed from the earth; and Noah only remained alive, and they that were with him in the ark.

And the waters prevailed upon the earth an hundred and fifty days.—*Genesis vii, 11 24.*

NOAH CURSING HAM

And the sons of Noah, that went forth of the ark, were Shem, and Ham, and Japheth; and Ham is the father of Canaan These *are* the three sons of Noah and of them was the whole earth overspread

And Noah began to be an husbandman, and he planted a vineyard And he drank of the wine, and was drunken, and he was uncovered within his tent And Ham, the father of Canaan, saw the nakedness of his father, and told his two brethren without And Shem and Japheth took a garment, and laid it upon both their shoulders, and went backward, and covered the nakedness of their father, and their faces were backward, and they saw not their father's nakedness And Noah awoke from his wine, and knew what his younger son had done unto him And he said, Cursed be Canaan, a servant of servants shall he be unto his brethren And he said, Blessed be the Lord God of Shem, and Canaan shall be his servant God shall enlarge Japheth, and he shall dwell in the tents of Shem; and Canaan shall be his servant —*Genesis ix, 18–27.*

THE TOWER OF BABEL

And the whole earth was of one language, and of one speech.

And it came to pass as they journeyed from the east, that they found a plain in the land of Shinar, and they dwelt there And they said one to another, Go to, let us make brick, and burn them thoroughly And they had brick for stone, and slime had they for mortar And they said, Go to, let us build us a city and a tower, whose top may reach unto heaven, and let us make us a name, lest we be scattered abroad upon the face of the whole earth

And the Lord came down to see the city and the tower which the children of men builded And the Lord said, Behold, the people is one, and they have all one language, and this they begin to do: and now nothing will be restrained from them, which they have imagined to do. Go to, let us go down, and there confound their language, that they may not understand one another's speech

So the Lord scattered them abroad from thence upon the face of all the earth and they left off to build the city

Therefore is the name of it called Babel, because the Lord did there confound the language of all the earth and from thence did the Lord scatter them abroad upon the face of all the earth.—*Genesis xi, 1–9*

ABRAHAM ENTERTAINS THREE STRANGERS

In the selfsame day was Abraham circumcised, and Ishmael his son And all the men of his house, born in the house, and bought with money of the stranger, were circumcised with him.

And the Lord appeared unto him in the plains of Mamre. and he sat in the tent door in the heat of the day; and he lift up his eyes and looked, and, lo, three men stood by him and when he saw them, he ran to meet them from the tent door, and bowed himself toward the ground, and said, My Lord, if now I have found favour in thy sight, pass not away, I pray thee, from thy servant let a little water, I pray you, be fetched, and wash your feet, and rest yourselves under the tree. And I will fetch a morsel of bread, and comfort ye your hearts; after that ye shall pass on for therefore are ye come to your servant. And they said, So do, as thou hast said

And Abraham hastened into the tent unto Sarah, and said, Make ready quickly three measures of fine meal, knead it, and make cakes upon the hearth And Abraham ran unto the herd, and fetched a calf tender and good, and gave it unto a young man, and he hasted to dress it And he took butter, and milk, and the calf which he had dressed, and set it before them, and he stood by them under the tree, and they did eat —*Genesis xvii, 26, 27; xviii, 1–8*

Be not forgetful to entertain strangers for thereby some have entertained angels unawares —*Hebrews xiii, 2*

THE DESTRUCTION OF SODOM.

And when the morning arose, then the angels hastened Lot, saying, Arise, take thy wife, and thy two daughters, which are here; lest thou be consumed in the iniquity of the city. And while he lingered, the men laid hold upon his hand, and upon the hand of his wife, and upon the hand of his two daughters; the Lord being merciful unto him: and they brought him forth, and set him without the city.

And it came to pass, when they had brought them forth abroad, that he said, Escape for thy life; look not behind thee, neither stay thou in all the plain; escape to the mountain, lest thou be consumed. And Lot said unto them, Oh, not so, my Lord. Behold now, thy servant hath found grace in thy sight, and thou hast magnified thy mercy, which thou hast shewed unto me in saving my life; and I cannot escape to the mountain, lest some evil take me and I die. Behold now this city is near to flee unto, and it is a little one: Oh, let me escape thither (is it not a little one?), and my soul shall live. And he said unto him, See, I have accepted thee concerning this thing also, that I will not overthrow this city, for the which thou hast spoken. Haste thee, escape thither; for I cannot do anything till thou be come thither. Therefore the name of the city was called Zoar.

The sun was risen upon the earth when Lot entered unto Zoar. Then the Lord rained upon Sodom and upon Gomorrah brimstone and fire from the Lord out of heaven; and he overthrew those cities, and all the plain, and all the inhabitants of the cities, and that which grew upon the ground.

But his wife looked back from behind him, and she became a pillar of salt.

And Abraham gat up early in the morning to the place where he stood before the Lord: and he looked toward Sodom and Gomorrah, and toward all the land of the plain, and beheld, and lo, the smoke of the country went up as the smoke of a furnace.—*Genesis xix, 15-28.*

G. Doré

THE EXPULSION OF HAGAR.

And the Lord visited Sarah as he had said, and the Lord did unto Sarah as he had spoken For Sarah conceived, and bare Abraham a son in his old age, at the set time of which God had spoken to him And Abraham called the name of his son that was born unto him, whom Sarah bare to him, Isaac And Abraham circumcised his son Isaac, being eight days old, as God had commanded him And Abraham was an hundred years old, when his son Isaac was born unto him

And Sarah said, God hath made me to laugh, so that all that hear will laugh with me And she said, Who would have said unto Abraham, that Sarah should have given children suck? for I have born him a son in his old age And the child grew, and was weaned and Abraham made a great feast the same day that Isaac was weaned

And Sarah saw the son of Hagar, the Egyptian, which she had born unto Abraham, mocking Wherefore she said unto Abraham, Cast out this bondwoman and her son; for the son of this bondwoman shall not be heir with my son, even with Isaac.

And the thing was very grievous in Abraham's sight because of his son And God said unto Abraham, Let it not be grievous in thy sight because of the lad, and because of thy bondwoman, in all that Sarah hath said unto thee, hearken unto her voice, for in Isaac shall thy seed be called And also of the son of the bondwoman will I make a nation, because he is thy seed

And Abraham rose up early in the morning, and took bread, and a bottle of water, and gave it unto Hagar, putting it on her shoulder, and the child, and sent her away and she departed, and wandered in the wilderness of Beer-sheba —*Genesis xxi, 1–14*

G. Doré

THE TRIAL OF THE FAITH OF ABRAHAM

And it came to pass after these things, that God did tempt Abraham, and said unto him, Abraham: and he said, Behold, here I am And he said, Take now thy son, thine only son Isaac, whom thou lovest, and get thee into the land of Moriah; and offer him there for a burnt offering upon one of the mountains which I will tell thee of

And Abraham rose up early in the morning, and saddled his ass, and took two of his young men with him, and Isaac his son, and clave the wood for the burnt offering, and rose up and went unto the place of which God had told him Then on the third day Abraham lifted up his eyes and saw the place afar off And Abraham said unto his young men, Abide ye here with the ass; and I and the lad will go yonder and worship, and come again to you. And Abraham took the wood of the burnt offering and laid it upon Isaac his son; and he took the fire in his hand and a knife, and they went both of them together And Isaac spake unto Abraham his father, and said, My father and he said, Here am I, my son And he said, Behold the fire and the wood but where is the lamb for a burnt offering? And Abraham said, My son, God will provide himself a lamb for a burnt offering: so they went both of them together And they came to the place which God had told him of; and Abraham built an altar there, and laid the wood in order, and bound Isaac his son, and laid him on the altar upon the wood And Abraham stretched forth his hand and took the knife to slay his son And the angel of the Lord called unto him out of heaven, and said, Abraham, Abraham and he said, Here am I. And he said, Lay not thine hand upon the lad, neither do thou anything unto him for now I know that thou fearest God, seeing thou hast not withheld thy son, thine only son, from me And Abraham lifted up his eyes and looked, and behold behind him a ram caught in a thicket by his horns: and Abraham went and took the ram, and offered him up for a burnt offering in the stead of his son.

And Abraham called the name of that place Jehovah-jireh as it is to this day, In the mount of the Lord it shall be seen.

And the angel of the Lord called unto Abraham out of heaven the second time, and said, By myself have I sworn, saith the Lord, for because thou hast done this thing, and hast not withheld thy son, thine only son, that in blessing I will bless thee, and in multiplying I will multiply thy seed as the stars of heaven, and as the sand which is upon the sea shore; and thy seed shall possess the gate of his enemies; and in thy seed shall all the nations of the earth be blessed, because thou hast obeyed my voice.—*Genesis xxii 1–18*

THE BURIAL OF SARAH.

And Sarah was an hundred and seven and twenty years old. these were the years of the life of Sarah. And Sarah died in Kirjath-arba; the same is Hebron in the land of Canaan: and Abraham came to mourn for Sarah, and to weep for her.

And Abraham stood up from before his dead, and spake unto the sons of Heth, saying, I am a stranger and a sojourner with you: give me a possession of a buryingplace with you, that I may bury my dead out of my sight.

And the children of Heth answered Abraham, saying unto him, Hear us, my lord: thou art a mighty prince among us: in the choice of our sepulchres bury thy dead; none of us shall withhold from thee his sepulchre, but that thou mayest bury thy dead.

And Abraham stood up, and bowed himself to the people of the land, even to the children of Heth. And he communed with them, saying, If it be your mind that I should bury my dead out of my sight; hear me, and intreat for me to Ephron the son of Zohar, that he may give me the cave of Machpelah, which he hath, which is in the end of his field; for as much money as it is worth he shall give it me for a possession of a buryingplace amongst you.

And Ephron dwelt among the children of Heth: and Ephron the Hittite answered Abraham in the audience of the children of Heth, even of all that went in at the gate of his city, saying, Nay, my lord, hear me: the field give I thee, and the cave that is therein, I give it thee; in the presence of the sons of my people give I it thee: bury thy dead.

And Abraham bowed down himself before the people of the land. And he spake unto Ephron in the audience of the people of the land, saying, But if thou wilt give it, I pray thee, hear me: I will give thee money for the field; take it of me, and I will bury my dead there.

And Ephron answered Abraham, saying unto him, My lord, hearken unto me: the land is worth four hundred shekels of silver: what is that betwixt me and thee? bury therefore thy dead.

And Abraham hearkened unto Ephron; and Abraham weighed to Ephron the silver, which he had named in the audience of the sons of Heth, four hundred shekels of silver, current money with the merchant.

And the field of Ephron, which was in Machpelah, which was before Mamre, the field, and the cave which was therein, and all the trees that were in the field, that were in all the borders round about, were made sure unto Abraham for a possession in the presence of the children of Heth, before all that went in at the gate of his city.

And after this, Abraham buried Sarah his wife in the cave of the field of Machpelah before Mamre; the same is Hebron in the land of Canaan. And the field, and the cave that is therein, were made sure unto Abraham for a possession of a buryingplace by the sons of Heth.—*Genesis xxiii.*

ELIEZER AND REBEKAH.

And the servant put his hand under the thigh of Abraham his master, and sware to him concerning that matter.

And the servant took ten camels of the camels of his master, and departed; for all the goods of his master were in his hand: and he arose and went to Mesopotamia, unto the city of Nahor. And he made his camels to kneel down, without the city by a well of water at the time of the evening, even the time that women go out to draw water. And he said, O Lord God of my master Abraham, I pray thee, send me good speed this day, and shew kindness unto my master Abraham. Behold, I stand here by the well of water; and the daughters of the men of the city come out to draw water: and let it come to pass, that the damsel to whom I shall say, Let down thy pitcher, I pray thee, that I may drink; and she shall say, Drink, and I will give thy camels drink also: let the same be she that thou hast appointed for thy servant Isaac; and thereby shall I know that thou hast shewed kindness unto my master.

And it came to pass before he had done speaking, that, behold, Rebekah came out, who was born to Bethuel, son of Milcah, the wife of Nahor, Abraham's brother, with her pitcher upon her shoulder. And the damsel was very fair to look upon, a virgin, neither had any man known her: and she went down to the well, and filled her pitcher and came up. And the servant ran to meet her, and said, Let me, I pray thee, drink a little water of thy pitcher. And she said, Drink, my lord; and she hasted, and let down her pitcher upon her hand, and gave him drink. And when she had done giving him drink, she said, I will draw water for thy camels also, until they have done drinking. And she hasted and emptied her pitcher into the trough, and ran again unto the well to draw water, and drew for all his camels.

And the man wondering at her held his peace, to wit whether the Lord had made his journey prosperous or not.

And it came to pass, as the camels had done drinking, that the man took a golden earring of half a shekel weight, and two bracelets for her hands of ten shekels weight of gold: and said, Whose daughter art thou? tell me, I pray thee; is there room in thy father's house for us to lodge in? And she said unto him, I am the daughter of Bethuel the son of Milcah, which she bare unto Nahor. She said moreover unto him, We have both straw and provender enough, and room to lodge in.

And the man bowed down his head and worshiped the Lord. And he said, Blessed be the Lord God of my master Abraham, who hath not left destitute my master of his mercy and his truth: I being in the way, the Lord led me to the house of my master's brethren.

And the damsel ran, and told them of her mother's house these things.—*Genesis xxiv, 9–28.*

ISAAC BLESSING JACOB.

And it came to pass, that when Isaac was old, and his eyes were dim, so that he could not see, he called Esau, his eldest son, and said unto him, My son: and he said unto him, Behold, here am I. And he said, Behold now, I am old, I know not the day of my death: Now therefore take, I pray thee, thy weapons, thy quiver and thy bow, and go out to the field, and take me some venison; And make me savoury meat, such as I love, and bring it to me, that I may eat; that my soul may bless thee before I die.

And Rebekah heard when Isaac spake to Esau his son. And Esau went to the field to hunt for venison, and to bring it.

And Rebekah spake unto Jacob her son, saying, Behold, I heard thy father speak unto Esau thy brother, saying, Bring me venison, and make me savoury meat, that I may eat, and bless thee before the Lord before my death. Now therefore, my son, obey my voice according to that which I command thee. Go now to the flock, and fetch me from thence two good kids of the goats; and I will make them savoury meat for thy father such as he loveth; And thou shalt bring it to thy father, that he may eat, and that he may bless thee before his death.

And Jacob said to Rebekah his mother, Behold, Esau my brother is a hairy man, and I am a smooth man: My father peradventure will feel me, and I shall seem to him as a deceiver; and I shall bring a curse upon me, and not a blessing.

And his mother said unto him, Upon me be thy curse, my son: only obey my voice, and go fetch me them.

And he went, and fetched, and brought them to his mother: and his mother made savoury meat, such as his father loved. And Rebekah took goodly raiment of her eldest son Esau, which were with her in the house, and put them upon Jacob her younger son: And she put the skins of the kids of the goats upon his hands and upon the smooth of his neck: And she gave the savoury meat and the bread, which she had prepared, into the hand of her son Jacob.

And he came unto his father, and said, My father: and he said, Here am I; who art thou, my son? And Jacob said unto his father, I am Esau thy first born; I have done according as thou badest me: arise, I pray thee, sit and eat of my venison, that thy soul may bless me. And Isaac said unto his son, How is it that thou hast found it so quickly, my son? And he said, Because the Lord thy God brought it to me. And Isaac said unto Jacob, Come near, I pray thee, that I may feel thee, my son, whether thou be my very son Esau or not. And Jacob went near unto Isaac his father; and he felt him, and said, The voice is Jacob's voice, but the hands are the hands of Esau. And he discerned him not, because his hands were hairy, as his brother Esau's hands: so he blessed him.

And he said, Art thou my very son Esau? And he said, I am. And he said, Bring it near to me, and I will eat of my son's venison, that my soul may bless thee. And he brought it near to him, and he did eat; and he brought him wine, and he drank. And his father Isaac said unto him, Come near now, and kiss me, my son. And he came near, and kissed him: and he smelled the smell of his raiment, and blessed him, and said, See, the smell of my son is as the smell of a field which the Lord hath blessed: Therefore God give thee of the dew of heaven, and the fatness of the earth, and plenty of corn and wine: Let people serve thee, and nations bow down to thee: be lord over thy brethren, and let thy mother's sons bow down to thee: cursed be every one that curseth thee, and blessed be he that blesseth thee.—*Genesis xxvii, 1–29.*

JACOB TENDING THE FLOCKS OF LABAN.

And while he yet spake with them, Rachel came with her father's sheep for she kept them And it came to pass, when Jacob saw Rachel the daughter of Laban his mother's brother, and the sheep of Laban his mother's brother, that Jacob went near, and rolled the stone from the well's mouth, and watered the flock of Laban his mother's brother And Jacob kissed Rachel, and lifted up his voice, and wept And Jacob told Rachel that he was her father's brother, and that he was Rebekah's son and she ran and told her father

And it came to pass, when Laban heard the tidings of Jacob his sister's son, that he ran to meet him, and embraced him, and kissed him, and brought him to his house And he told Laban all these things. And Laban said to him, Surely thou art my bone and my flesh And he abode with him the space of a month And Laban said unto Jacob, Because thou art my brother, shouldest thou therefore serve me for naught? tell me, what shall thy wages be?

And Laban had two daughters the name of the elder was Leah, and the name of the younger was Rachel Leah was tender eyed, but Rachel was beautiful and well favoured

And Jacob loved Rachel, and said, I will serve thee seven years for Rachel thy younger daughter And Laban said, It is better that I give her to thee, than that I should give her to another man, abide with me

And Jacob served seven years for Rachel, and they seemed unto him but a few days, for the love he had for her And Jacob said unto Laban, Give me my wife, for my days are fulfilled, that I may go in unto her

And Laban gathered together all the men of the place, and made a feast And it came to pass in the evening, that he took Leah his daughter, and brought her to him, and he went in unto her And Laban gave unto his daughter Leah Zilpah his maid, for an handmaid And it came to pass that in the morning, behold, it was Leah and he said to Laban, What is this thou hast done unto me? did not I serve with thee for Rachel? wherefore then hast thou beguiled me? And Laban said, It must not be so done in our country, to give the younger before the firstborn Fulfil her week, and we will give thee this also for the service which thou shalt serve with me yet seven other years

And Jacob did so, and fulfilled her week, and he gave him Rachel his daughter to wife also And Laban gave to Rachel his daughter Bilhah his handmaid to be her maid And he went in also unto Rachel, and he loved also Rachel more than Leah, and served with him yet seven other years —*Genesis xxix, 9–30*

JOSEPH SOLD INTO EGYPT

These are the generations of Jacob Joseph, being seventeen years old, was feeding the flock with his brethren, and the lad was with the sons of Bilhah and with the sons of Zilpah, his father's wives, and Joseph brought unto his father their evil report Now Israel loved Joseph more than all his children, because he was the son of his old age, and he made him a coat of many colors And when his brethren saw that their father loved him more than all his brethren, they hated him, and could not speak peaceably unto him

And Joseph dreamed a dream, and he told it his brethren. and they hated him yet the more And he said unto them, Hear, I pray you, this dream which I have dreamed For, behold, we were binding sheaves in the field, and, lo, my sheaf arose, and also stood upright, and, behold, your sheaves stood round about, and made obeisance to my sheaf And his brethren said to him, Shalt thou indeed reign over us? or shalt thou indeed have dominion over us? And they hated him yet the more for his dreams and for his words

And he dreamed yet another dream, and told it his brethren, and said, Behold, I have dreamed a dream more, and, behold, the sun and the moon and the eleven stars made obeisance to me And he told it to his father and to his brethren, and his father rebuked him, and said unto him, What is this dream that thou hast dreamed? Shall I and thy mother and thy brethren indeed come to bow down ourselves to thee to the earth. And his brethren envied him, but his father observed the saying

And his brethren went to feed their father's flock in Shechem

And Joseph went after his brethren, and found them in Dothan And when they saw him afar off, even before he came near unto them, they conspired against him to slay him And they said one to another, Behold, this dreamer cometh. Come now, therefore, and let us slay him, and cast him into some pit, and we will say, Some evil beast hath devoured him, and we shall see what will become of his dreams And Reuben heard it, and he delivered him out of their hands, and said, Let us not kill him And Reuben said unto them, Shed no blood, but cast him into this pit that is in the wilderness, and lay no hand upon him, that he might rid him out of their hands to deliver him to his father again

And it came to pass, when Joseph was come unto his brethren, that they stript Joseph out of his coat, his coat of many colors that was on him, and they took him and cast him into a pit, and the pit was empty, there was no water in it And they sat down to eat bread, and they lifted up their eyes and looked, and, behold, a company of Ishmaelites came from Gilead with their camels bearing spicery and balm and myrrh, going to carry it down to Egypt And Judah said unto his brethren, What profit is it if we slay our brother, and conceal his blood? Come, and let us sell him to the Ishmaelites, and let not our hand be upon him, for he is our brother and our flesh And his brethren were content

Then there passed by Midianites merchantmen, and they drew and lifted up Joseph out of the pit, and sold Joseph to the Ishmaelites for twenty pieces of silver, and they brought Joseph into Egypt

And the Midianites sold him into Egypt unto Potiphar, an officer of Pharaoh's, and captain of the guard —*Genesis xxxvii, 2–12, 17–28, 36.*

G. Doré

JOSEPH INTERPRETING PHARAOH'S DREAM

And it came to pass at the end of two full years, that Pharaoh dreamed and, behold, he stood by the river And, behold, there came up out of the river seven well favoured kine and fatfleshed, and they fed in a meadow And, behold, seven other kine came up after them out of the river, ill favoured and leanfleshed, and stood by the other kine upon the brink of the river And the ill favored and leanfleshed kine did eat up the seven well favoured and fat kine So Pharaoh awoke

And he slept and dreamed the second time · and, behold, seven ears of corn came up upon one stalk, rank and good. And, behold, seven thin ears and blasted with the east wind sprung up after them And the seven thin ears devoured the seven rank and full ears And Pharaoh awoke, and, behold, it was a dream

And it came to pass in the morning that his spirit was troubled, and he sent and called for all the magicians of Egypt, and all the wise men thereof · and Pharaoh told them his dream, but there was none that could interpret them unto Pharaoh.

[At the suggestion of his chief butler Pharaoh sends for Joseph and relates to him his dreams, which Joseph interprets as follows]

And Joseph said unto Pharaoh, The dream of Pharaoh is one God hath shewed Pharaoh what he is about to do The seven good kine are seven years; and the seven good ears are seven years the dream is one And the seven thin and ill favoured kine that came up after them are seven years, and the seven empty ears blasted with the east wind shall be seven years of famine This is the thing which I have spoken unto Pharaoh · What God is about to do he sheweth unto Pharaoh Behold, there come seven years of great plenty throughout all the land of Egypt: And there shall arise after them seven years of famine, and all the plenty shall be forgotten in the land of Egypt, and the famine shall consume the land, and the plenty shall not be known in the land by reason of that famine following, for it shall be very grievous And for that the dream was doubled unto Pharaoh twice · it is because the thing is established by God, and God will shortly bring it to pass

Now therefore let Pharaoh look out a man discreet and wise, and set him over the land of Egypt. Let Pharaoh do this, and let him appoint officers over the land, and take up the fifth part of the land of Egypt in the seven plenteous years And let them gather all the food of those good years that come, and lay up corn under the hand of Pharaoh, and let them keep food in the cities And that food shall be for store to the land against the seven years of famine, which shall be in the land of Egypt, that the land perish not through the famine —*Genesis xli, 1–36.*

JOSEPH MAKING HIMSELF KNOWN TO HIS BRETHREN

Then Joseph could not refrain himself before all them that stood by him, and he cried, Cause every man to go out from me And there stood no man with him, while Joseph made himself known unto his brethren And he wept aloud and the Egyptians and the house of Pharaoh heard

And Joseph said unto his brethren, I am Joseph; doth my father yet live? And his brethren could not answer him, for they were troubled at his presence And Joseph said unto his brethren, Come near to me, I pray you And they came near And he said, I am Joseph your brother, whom ye sold into Egypt Now therefore be not grieved, nor angry with yourselves, that ye sold me hither for God did send me before you to preserve life For these two years hath the famine been in the land. and yet there are five years, in which there shall neither be earing nor harvest. And God sent me before you to preserve you a posterity in the earth, and to save your lives by a great deliverance So now it was not you that sent me hither, but God and he hath made me a father to Pharaoh, and lord of all his house, and a ruler throughout all the land of Egypt Haste ye, and go up to my father, and say unto him, Thus saith thy son Joseph, God hath made me lord of all Egypt come down unto me, tarry not And thou shalt dwell in the land of Goshen, and thou shalt be near unto me, thou, and thy children, and thy children's children, and thy flocks, and thy herds, and all that thou hast And there will I nourish thee, for yet there are five years of famine, lest thou, and thy household, and all that thou hast, come to poverty And, behold, your eyes see, and the eyes of my brother Benjamin, that it is my mouth that speaketh unto you. And ye shall tell my father of all my glory in Egypt, and of all that ye have seen, and ye shall haste and bring down my father hither

And he fell upon his brother Benjamin's neck, and wept, and Benjamin wept upon his neck. Moreover he kissed all his brethren, and wept upon them. and after that his brethren talked with him

And the fame thereof was heard in Pharaoh's house, saying, Joseph's brethren are come and it pleased Pharaoh well, and his servants

And Pharaoh said unto Joseph, say unto thy brethren, This do ye; lade your beasts, and go, get you unto the land of Canaan; and take your father and your households, and come unto me and I will give you the good of the land of Egypt, and ye shall eat the fat of the land — *Genesis xlv, 1–18.*

MOSES IN THE BULRUSHES

And there went a man of the house of Levi, and took to wife a daughter of Levi And the woman conceived, and bare a son and when she saw him that he was a goodly child, she hid him three months And when she could not longer hide him, she took for him an ark of bulrushes, and daubed it with slime and with pitch, and put the child therein, and she laid it in the flags by the river's brink And his sister stood afar off, to wit what would be done to him

And the daughter of Pharaoh came down to wash herself at the river, and her maidens walked along by the river's side; and when she saw the ark among the flags, she sent her maid to fetch it And when she had opened it, she saw the child. and, behold, the babe wept And she had compassion on him, and said, This is one of the Hebrews' children Then said his sister to Pharaoh's daughter, Shall I go and call to thee a nurse of the Hebrew women, that she may nurse the child for thee? And Pharaoh's daughter said to her, Go And the maid went and called the child's mother And Pharaoh's daughter said unto her, Take this child away, and nurse it for me, and I will give thee thy wages And the woman took the child and nursed it

And the child grew, and she brought him unto Pharaoh's daughter, and he became her son And she called his name Moses and she said, Because I drew him out of the water
—*Exodus ii, 1–10.*

G. Doré

THE WAR AGAINST GIBEON.

Therefore the five kings of the Amorites, the king of Jerusalem, the king of Hebron, the king of Jarmuth, the king of Lachish, the king of Eglon, gathered themselves together, and went up, they and all their hosts, and encamped before Gibeon, and made war against it

And the men of Gibeon sent unto Joshua to the camp to Gilgal, saying, Slack not thy hand from thy servants, come up to us quickly, and save us and help us for all the kings of the Amorites that dwell in the mountains are gathered together against us

So Joshua ascended from Gilgal, he, and all the people of war with him, and all the mighty men of valor. And the Lord said unto Joshua, Fear them not for I have delivered them into thine hand, there shall not a man of them stand before thee. Joshua therefore came unto them suddenly, and went up from Gilgal all night And the Lord discomfited them before Israel, and slew them with a great slaughter at Gibeon, and chased them along the way that goeth up to Beth-horon, and smote them to Azekah, and unto Makkedah. And it came to pass, as they fled from before Israel, and were in the going down to Beth-horon, that the Lord cast down great stones from heaven upon them unto Azekah, and they died · they were more which died with hailstones than they whom the children of Israel slew with the sword.

Then spake Joshua to the Lord in the day when the Lord delivered up the Amorites before the children of Israel, and he said in the sight of Israel, Sun, stand thou still upon Gibeon; and thou, Moon, in the valley of Ajalon And the sun stood still, and the moon stayed, until the people had avenged themselves upon their enemies. Is not this written in the book of Jasher? So the sun stood still in the midst of heaven, and hastened not to go down about a whole day And there was no day like that before it or after it, that the Lord hearkened unto the voice of a man. for the Lord fought for Israel

And Joshua returned, and all Israel with him, unto the camp to Gilgal. But these five kings fled, and hid themselves in a cave at Makkedah And it was told Joshua, saying, The five kings are found hid in a cave at Makkedah And Joshua said, Roll great stones upon the mouth of the cave, and set men by it for to keep them and stay ye not, but pursue after your enemies, and smite the hindmost of them; suffer them not to enter into their cities, for the Lord your God hath delivered them into your hand.

And it came to pass, when Joshua and the children of Israel had made an end of slaying them with a very great slaughter, till they were consumed, that the rest which remained of them entered into fenced cities —*Joshua x, 5–20*

SISERA SLAIN BY JAEL.

Now Heber the Kenite, which was of the children of Hobab, the father-in-law of Moses, had severed himself from the Kenites, and pitched his tent unto the plain of Zaanaim, which is by Kedesh.

And they shewed Sisera that Barak, the son of Abinoam, was gone up to Mount Tabor. And Sisera gathered together all his chariots, even nine hundred chariots of iron, and all the people that were with him, from Harosheth of the Gentiles unto the river of Kishon.

And Deborah said unto Barak, Up; for this is the day in which the Lord hath delivered Sisera into thine hand: is not the Lord gone out before thee? So Barak went down from Mount Tabor, and ten thousand men after him.

And the Lord discomfited Sisera, and all his chariots and all his host, with the edge of the sword before Barak; so that Sisera lighted down off his chariot, and fled away on his feet. But Barak pursued after the chariots, and after the host, unto Harosheth of the Gentiles: and all the host of Sisera fell upon the edge of the sword; and there was not a man left.

Howbeit Sisera fled away on his feet to the tent of Jael, the wife of Heber the Kenite; for there was peace between Jabin the king of Hazor and the house of Heber the Kenite. And Jael went out to meet Sisera, and said unto him, Turn in, my lord, turn in to me; fear not. And when he had turned in unto her into the tent, she covered him with a mantle. And he said unto her, Give me, I pray thee, a little water to drink; for I am thirsty. And she opened a bottle of milk, and gave him drink, and covered him. Again he said unto her, Stand in the door of the tent, and it shall be, when any man doth come and enquire of thee, and say, Is there any man here? that thou shalt say, No. Then Jael, Heber's wife, took a nail of the tent, and took an hammer in her hand, and went softly unto him, and smote the nail into his temples, and fastened it into the ground: for he was fast asleep and weary. So he died.

And, behold, as Barak pursued Sisera, Jael came out to meet him, and said unto him, Come, and I will show thee the man whom thou seekest. And when he came into her tent, behold, Sisera lay dead, and the nail was in his temples.—*Judges iv, 11–22.*

DEBORAH'S SONG OF TRIUMPH

Then sang Deborah and Barak, the son of Abinoam on that day, saying —

Praise ye the Lord for the avenging of Israel,
When the people willingly offered themselves
Hear, O ye kings, give ear, O ye princes,
I, even I, will sing unto the Lord,
I will sing praise to the Lord God of Israel
Lord, when thou wentest out of Seir,
When thou marchedst out of the field of Edom,
The earth trembled, and the heavens dropped, the clouds also dropped water
The mountains melted from before the Lord,
Even that Sinai from before the Lord God of Israel

* * * * * *

Blessed above women shall Jael the wife of Heber the Kenite be,
Blessed shall she be above women in the tent
He asked water, and she gave him milk,
She brought forth butter in a lordly dish
She put her hand to the nail, and her right hand to the workmen's hammer,
And with the hammer she smote Sisera,
She smote off his head, when she had pierced and stricken through his temples
At her feet he bowed, he fell, he lay down
At her feet he bowed, he fell
Where he bowed, there he fell down dead
The mother of Sisera looked out at a window, and cried through the lattice,
Why is his chariot so long in coming? Why tarry the wheels of his chariots?
Her wise ladies answered her, yea, she returned answer to herself,
Have they not sped? Have they not divided the prey,
To every man a damsel or two,
To Sisera a prey of divers colours, a prey of divers colours of needlework,
Of divers colours of needlework on both sides, meet for the necks of them that take the spoil?
So let all thine enemies perish, O Lord
But let them that love him be as the sun when he goeth forth in his might

Judges v, 2–5, 24–31

JEPHTHAH MET BY HIS DAUGHTER

Then the Spirit of the Lord came upon Jephthah, and he passed over Gilead, and Manasseh, and passed over Mizpeh of Gilead, and from Mizpeh of Gilead he passed over unto the children of Ammon

And Jephthah vowed a vow unto the Lord, and said, If thou shalt without fail deliver the children of Ammon into mine hands, then it shall be, that whatsoever cometh forth of the doors of my house to meet me, when I return in peace from the children of Ammon, shall surely be the Lord's, and I will offer it up for a burnt offering

So Jephthah passed over unto the children of Ammon to fight against them ; and the Lord delivered them into his hands And he smote them from Aroer, even till thou come to Minnith, even twenty cities, and unto the plain of the vineyards, with a very great slaughter Thus the children of Ammon were subdued before the children of Israel

And Jephthah came to Mizpeh unto his house, and, behold, his daughter came out to meet him with timbrels and with dances and she was his only child , beside her he had neither son nor daughter —*Judges xi, 29–34*

JEPHTHAH'S DAUGHTER AND HER COMPANIONS

And it came to pass, when he saw her, that he rent his clothes, and said, Alas, my daughter! thou hast brought me very low, and thou art one of them that trouble me: for I have opened my mouth unto the Lord, and I cannot go back.

And she said unto him, My father, if thou hast opened thy mouth unto the Lord, do to me according to that which hath proceeded out of thy mouth; forasmuch as the Lord hath taken vengeance for thee of thine enemies, even of the children of Ammon. And she said unto her father, Let this thing be done for me: let me alone two months, that I may go up and down upon the mountains, and bewail my virginity, I and my fellows.

And he said, Go. And he sent her away for two months: and she went with her companions, and bewailed her virginity upon the mountains.

And it came to pass at the end of two months, that she returned unto her father, who did with her according to his vow which he had vowed: and she knew no man.

And it was a custom in Israel, that the daughters of Israel went yearly to lament the daughter of Jephthah the Gileadite four days in a year.—*Judges xi, 35-40.*

SAMSON SLAYING THE LION.

Then went Samson down, and his father and his mother, to Timnath, and came to the vineyards of Timnath; and, behold, a young lion roared against him. And the Spirit of the Lord came mightily upon him, and he rent him as he would have rent a kid, and he had nothing in his hand; but he told not his father or his mother what he had done.—*Judges xiv, 5–6.*

SAMSON AND DELILAH.

And it came to pass afterward, that he loved a woman in the valley of Sorek, whose name was Delilah.

And the lords of the Philistines came up unto her, and said unto her, Entice him, and see wherein his great strength lieth, and by what means we may prevail against him, that we may bind him to afflict him; and we will give thee every one of us eleven hundred pieces of silver.

And Delilah said to Samson, Tell me, I pray thee, wherein thy great strength lieth, and wherewith thou mightest be bound to afflict thee. And Samson said unto her, If they bind me with seven green withs that were never dried, then shall I be weak, and be as another man. Then the lords of the Philistines brought up to her seven green withs which had not been dried, and she bound him with them. Now there were men lying in wait, abiding with her in the chamber. And she said unto him, The Philistines be upon thee, Samson. And he brake the withs, as a thread of tow is broken when it toucheth the fire. So his strength was not known.

And Delilah said unto Samson, Behold, thou hast mocked me, and told me lies: now tell me, I pray thee, wherewith thou mightest be bound. And he said unto her, If they bind me fast with new ropes that never were occupied, then shall I be weak, and be as another man. Delilah therefore took new ropes, and bound him therewith, and said unto him, The Philistines be upon thee, Samson. And there were liers in wait abiding in the chamber. And he brake them from off his arms like a thread.

And Delilah said unto Samson, Hitherto thou hast mocked me, and told me lies: tell me wherewith thou mightest be bound. And he said unto her, If thou weavest the seven locks of my head with the web. And she fastened it with the pin, and said unto him, The Philistines be upon thee, Samson. And he awaked out of his sleep, and went away with the pin of the beam and with the web.

And she said unto him, How canst thou say, I love thee, when thine heart is not with me? thou hast mocked me these three times, and hast not told me wherein thy great strength lieth. And it came to pass, when she pressed him daily with her words, and urged him, so that his soul was vexed unto death; that he told her all his heart, and said unto her, There hath not come a razor upon mine head; for I have been a Nazarite unto God from my mother's womb: if I be shaven, then my strength will go from me, and I shall become weak, and be like any other man.

And when Delilah saw that he had told her all his heart, she sent and called for the lords of the Philistines, saying, Come up this once, for he hath showed me all his heart. Then the lords of the Philistines came up unto her, and brought money in their hand. And she made him sleep upon her knees; and she called for a man, and she caused him to shave off the seven locks of his head; and she began to afflict him, and his strength went from him. And she said, The Philistines be upon thee, Samson. And he awoke out of his sleep, and said, I will go out as at other times before, and shake myself. And he wist not that the Lord was departed from him.—*Judges xvi, 4–20.*

THE DEATH OF SAMSON

But the Philistines took him, and put out his eyes, and brought him down to Gaza, and bound him with fetters of brass, and he did grind in the prison house

Howbeit the hair of his head began to grow again after he was shaven

Then the lords of the Philistines gathered them together for to offer a great sacrifice unto Dagon their god, and to rejoice for they said, Our God hath delivered Samson our enemy into our hand And when the people saw him, they praised their god. for they said, Our god hath delivered into our hands our enemy, and the destroyer of our country, which slew many of us And it came to pass, when their hearts were merry, that they said, Call for Samson, that he may make us sport. And they called for Samson out of the prison house, and he made them sport and they set him between the pillars And Samson said unto the lad that held him by the hand, Suffer me that I may feel the pillars whereupon the house standeth, that I may lean upon them Now the house was full of men and women ; and all the lords of the Philistines were there, and there were upon the roof about three thousand men and women, that beheld while Samson made sport

And Samson called unto the Lord, and said, O Lord God, remember me, I pray thee, and strengthen me, I pray thee, only this once, O God, that I may be at once avenged of the Philistines for my two eyes And Samson took hold of the two middle pillars upon which the house stood, and on which it was borne up, of the one with his right hand, and of the other with his left And Samson said, Let me die with the Philistines And he bowed himself with all his might, and the house fell upon the lords, and upon all the people that were therein So the dead which he slew at his death were more than they which he slew in his life

Then his brethren and all the house of his father came down, and took him, and brought him up, and buried him between Zorah and Eshtaol in the buryingplace of Manoah his father And he judged Israel twenty years —*Judges xvi, 21–31.*

NAOMI AND HER DAUGHTERS IN LAW.

Now it came to pass in the days when the judges ruled, that there was a famine in the land. And a certain man of Beth-lehem-judah went to sojourn in the country of Moab, he, and his wife, and his two sons. And the name of the man was Elimelech, and the name of his wife Naomi, and the name of his two sons Mahlon and Chilion, Ephrathites of Beth-lehem-judah. And they came into the country of Moab, and continued there. And Elimelech Naomi's husband died; and she was left, and her two sons. And they took them wives of the women of Moab; the name of the one was Orpah, and the name of the other Ruth: and they dwelt there about ten years. And Mahlon and Chilion died also both of them; and the woman was left of her two sons and her husband.

Then she arose with her daughters in law, that she might return from the country of Moab: for she had heard in the country of Moab how that the Lord had visited his people in giving them bread. Wherefore she went forth out of the place where she was, and her two daughters in law with her; and they went on the way to return unto the land of Judah.

And Naomi said unto her two daughters in law, Go, return each to her mother's house: the Lord deal kindly with you, as ye have dealt with the dead, and with me. The Lord grant you that ye may find rest, each of you in the house of her husband.

Then she kissed them; and they lifted up their voice, and wept. And they said unto her, Surely we will return with thee unto thy people.

And Naomi said, Turn again, my daughters: why will ye go with me? are there yet any more sons in my womb, that they may be your husbands? Turn again, my daughters, go your way; for I am too old to have a husband. If I should say, I have hope, if I should have a husband also to night, and should also bear sons; would ye tarry for them till they were grown? would ye stay for them from having husbands? nay, my daughters; for it grieveth me much for your sakes that the hand of the Lord is gone out against me.

And they lifted up their voice, and wept again: and Orpah kissed her mother in law: but Ruth clave unto her.

And she said, Behold, thy sister in law is gone back unto her people, and unto her gods: return thou after thy sister in law.

And Ruth said, Entreat me not to leave thee, or to return from following after thee: for whither thou goest, I will go; and where thou lodgest, I will lodge: thy people shall be my people, and thy God my God: Where thou diest, will I die, and there will I be buried: the Lord do so to me, and more also, if ought but death part thee and me.

When she saw that she was steadfastly minded to go with her, then she left speaking unto her.

So they two went until they came to Beth-lehem.—*Ruth 1, 1–19.*

RUTH AND BOAZ.

And Naomi had a kinsman of her husband's, a mighty man of wealth, of the family of Elimelech; and his name was Boaz.

And Ruth the Moabitess said unto Naomi, Let me now go to the field, and glean ears of corn after him in whose sight I shall find grace. And she said unto her, Go, my daughter. And she went, and came and gleaned in the field after the reapers; and her hap was to light on a part of the field belonging unto Boaz, who was of the kindred of Elimelech.

And, behold, Boaz came from Bethlehem, and said unto the reapers, The Lord be with you. And they answered him, The Lord bless thee. Then said Boaz unto his servant that was set over the reapers, Whose damsel is this? And the servant that was set over the reapers answered and said, It is the Moabitish damsel that came back with Naomi out of the country of Moab: and she said, I pray you, let me glean and gather after the reapers among the sheaves: so she came, and hath continued even from the morning until now, that she tarried a little in the house.

Then said Boaz unto Ruth, Hearest thou not, my daughter? Go not to glean in another field, neither go from hence, but abide here fast by my maidens: let thine eyes be on the field that they do reap, and go thou after them: have I not charged the young men that they shall not touch thee? and when thou art athirst, go unto the vessels, and drink of that which the young men have drawn.

Then she fell on her face and bowed herself to the ground, and said unto him, Why have I found grace in thine eyes, that thou shouldest take knowledge of me, seeing I am a stranger?

And Boaz answered and said unto her, It hath fully been shewed me, all that thou hast done unto thy mother in law since the death of thine husband: and how thou hast left thy father and thy mother, and the land of thy nativity, and art come unto a people which thou knewest not heretofore. The Lord recompense thy work, and a full reward be given thee of the Lord God of Israel, under whose wings thou art come to trust.

Then she said, Let me find favor in thy sight, my lord; for that thou hast comforted me, and for that thou hast spoken friendly unto thine handmaid, though I be not like unto one of thine handmaidens.

And Boaz said unto her, At mealtime come thou hither, and eat of the bread, and dip thy morsel in the vinegar. And she sat beside the reapers: and he reached her parched corn, and she did eat, and was sufficed, and left. And when she was risen up to glean, Boaz commanded his young men, saying, Let her glean even among the sheaves, and reproach her not: and let fall also some of the handfuls of purpose for her, and leave them, that she may glean them and rebuke her not.

So she gleaned in the field until even, and beat out that she had gleaned: and it was about an ephah of barley.—*Ruth ii, 1–17.*

THE RETURN OF THE ARK.

And the ark of the Lord was in the country of the Philistines seven months. And the Philistines called for the priests and the diviners, saying, What shall we do to the ark of the Lord? tell us wherewith we shall send it to his place. And they said, If ye send away the ark of the God of Israel, send it not empty; but in any wise return him a trespass offering: then ye shall be healed, and it shall be known to you why his hand is not removed from you. Then said they, What shall be the trespass offering which we shall return to him? They answered, Five golden emerods, and five golden mice, according to the number of the lords of the Philistines: for one plague was on you all, and on your lords. Wherefore ye shall make images of your emerods, and images of your mice that mar the land; and ye shall give glory unto the God of Israel: peradventure he will lighten his hand from off you, and from off your gods, and from off your land. Wherefore then do ye harden your hearts, as the Egyptians and Pharaoh hardened their hearts? when he had wrought wonderfully among them, did they not let the people go, and they departed? Now therefore make a new cart, and take two milch kine, on which there hath come no yoke, and tie the kine to the cart, and bring their calves home from them: and take the ark of the Lord, and lay it upon the cart; and put the jewels of gold, which ye return him for a trespass offering, in a coffer by the side thereof; and send it away, that it may go. And see, if it goeth up by the way of his own coast to Beth-shemesh, then he hath done us this great evil: but if not, then we shall know that it is not his hand that smote us; it was a chance that happened to us.

And the men did so; and took two milch kine, and tied them to the cart, and shut up their calves at home: and they laid the ark of the Lord upon the cart, and the coffer with the mice of gold and the images of their emerods. And the kine took the straight way to the way of Beth-shemesh, and went along the highway, lowing as they went, and turned not aside to the right hand or to the left; and the lords of the Philistines went after them unto the border of Beth-shemesh. And they of Beth-shemesh were reaping their wheat harvest in the valley: and they lifted up their eyes, and saw the ark, and rejoiced to see it. And the cart came into the field of Joshua, a Beth-shemite, and stood there, where there was a great stone: and they clave the wood of the cart, and offered the kine a burnt offering unto the Lord.

And the Levites took down the ark of the Lord, and the coffer that was with it, wherein the jewels of gold were, and put them on the great stone: and the men of Beth-shemesh offered burnt offerings and sacrificed sacrifices the same day unto the Lord.—*1 Samuel vi, 1–15.*

SAUL AND DAVID

And it came to pass, when he had made an end of speaking unto Saul, that the soul of Jonathan was knit with the soul of David, and Jonathan loved him as his own soul And Saul took him that day, and would let him go no more home to his father's house

Then Jonathan and David made a covenant, because he loved him as his own soul And Jonathan stripped himself of the robe that was upon him, and gave it to David, and his garments, even to his sword, and to his bow, and to his girdle.

And David went out withersoever Saul sent him, and behaved himself wisely · and Saul set him over the men of war, and he was accepted in the sight of all the people, and also in the sight of Saul's servants

And it came to pass as they came, when David was returned from the slaughter of the Philistine, that the women came out of all cities of Israel, singing and dancing, to meet king Saul, with tabrets, with joy, and with instruments of music And the women answered one another as they played, and said, Saul hath slain his thousands, and David his ten thousands

And Saul was very wroth, and the saying displeased him, and he said, They have ascribed unto David ten thousands, and to me they have ascribed but thousands and what can he have more but the kingdom? And Saul eyed David from that day and forward

And it came to pass on the morrow, that the evil spirit from God came upon Saul, and he prophesied in the midst of the house and David played with his hand, as at other times and there was a javelin in Saul's hand And Saul cast the javelin, for he said, I will smite David even to the wall with it And David avoided out of his presence twice —*1 Samuel xviii, 1–11*

DAVID SPARING SAUL

And it came to pass, when Saul was returned from following the Philistines, that it was told him, saying, Behold, David is in the wilderness of En-gedi. Then Saul took three thousand chosen men out of all Israel, and went to seek David and his men upon the rocks of the wild goats. And he came to the sheep-cotes by the way, where was a cave; and Saul went in to cover his feet: and David and his men remained in the sides of the cave.

And the men of David said unto him, Behold the day of which the Lord said unto thee, Behold, I will deliver thine enemy into thine hand, that thou mayest do to him as it shall seem good unto thee. Then David arose, and cut off the skirt of Saul's robe privily. And it came to pass afterward, that David's heart smote him, because he had cut off Saul's skirt. And he said unto his men, The Lord forbid that I should do this thing unto my master, the Lord's anointed, to stretch forth mine hand against him, seeing he is the anointed of the Lord.

So David stayed his servants with these words, and suffered them not to rise against Saul. But Saul rose up out of the cave, and went on his way. David also arose afterward, and went out of the cave, and cried after Saul, saying, My lord the king. And when Saul looked behind him, David stooped with his face to the earth and bowed himself.

And David said to Saul, Wherefore hearest thou men's words, saying, Behold, David seeketh thy hurt? Behold, this day thine eyes have seen how that the Lord had delivered thee to-day into mine hand in the cave: and some bade me kill thee; but mine eye spared thee; and I said, I will not put forth mine hand against my lord; for he is the Lord's anointed. Moreover, my father, see, yea, see the skirt of thy robe in my hand: for in that I cut off the skirt of thy robe, and killed thee not, know thou and see that there is neither evil nor transgression in mine hand, and I have not sinned against thee; yet thou huntest my soul to take it. The Lord judge between me and thee, and the Lord avenge me of thee: but mine hand shall not be upon thee. As saith the proverb of the ancients, Wickedness proceedeth from the wicked: but mine hand shall not be upon thee. After whom is the king of Israel come out? after whom dost thou pursue? after a dead dog, after a flea. The Lord therefore be judge, and judge between me and thee, and see, and plead my cause, and deliver me out of thine hand.

And it came to pass, when David had made an end of speaking these words unto Saul, that Saul said, Is this thy voice, my son David? And Saul lifted up his voice, and wept. And he said to David, Thou art more righteous than I: for thou hast rewarded me good, whereas I have rewarded thee evil. And thou hast shewed this day how that thou hast dealt well with me: forasmuch as when the Lord had delivered me into thine hand, thou killedst me not. For if a man find his enemy, will he let him go well away? wherefore the Lord reward thee good for that thou hast done unto me this day. And now, behold, I know well that thou shalt surely be king, and that the kingdom of Israel shall be established in thine hand. Swear now therefore unto me by the Lord, that thou wilt not cut off my seed after me, and that thou wilt not destroy my name out of my father's house.

And David sware unto Saul. And Saul went home; but David and his men gat them up unto the hold.—*I Samuel xxiv, 1–22.*

DEATH OF SAUL

Now the Philistines fought against Israel and the men of Israel fled from before the Philistines, and fell down slain in mount Gilboa And the Philistines followed hard upon Saul and upon his sons, and the Philistines slew Jonathan, and Abinadab, and Melch-shua, Saul's sons

And the battle went sore against Saul, and the archers hit him, and he was sore wounded of the archers Then said Saul unto his armourbearer, Draw thy sword, and thrust me through therewith, lest these uncircumcised come and thrust me through, and abuse me But his armourbearer would not, for he was sore afraid Therefore Saul took a sword, and fell upon it And when his armourbearer saw that Saul was dead, he fell likewise upon his sword, and died with him

So Saul died, and his three sons, and his armourbearer, and all his men, that same day together

And when the men of Israel that were on the other side of the valley, and they that were on the other side Jordan, saw that the men of Israel fled, and that Saul and his sons were dead, they forsook the cities, and fled, and the Philistines came and dwelt in them And it came to pass on the morrow, when the Philistines came to strip the slain, that they found Saul and his three sons fallen in mount Gilboa. And they cut off his head, and stripped off his armour, and sent into the land of the Philistines round about, to publish it in the house of their idols, and among the people And they put his armour in the house of Ashtaroth: and they fastened his body to the wall of Beth-shan

And when the inhabitants of Jabesh-gilead heard of that which the Philistines had done to Saul, all the valiant men arose, and went all night, and took the body of Saul and the bodies of his sons from the wall of Beth-shan, and came to Jabesh, and burnt them there And they took their bones, and buried them under a tree at Jabesh, and fasted seven days—*1 Samuel xxxi.*

G. Doré

THE DEATH OF ABSALOM

And David numbered the people that were with him, and set captains of thousands and captains of hundreds over them And David set forth a third part of the people under the hand of Joab, and a third part under the hand of Abishai the son of Zeruiah, Joab's brother, and a third part under the hand of Ittai the Gittite And the king said unto the people, I will surely go forth with you myself also

But the people answered, Thou shalt not go forth for if we flee away, they will not care for us, neither if half of us die, will they care for us but now thou art worth ten thousand of us therefore now it is better that thou succor us out of the city

And the king said unto them, What seemeth you best I will do And the king stood by the gate side, and all the people came out by hundreds and by thousands And the king commanded Joab and Abishai and Ittai, saying, Deal gently for my sake with the young man even with Absalom And all the people heard when the king gave all the captains charge concerning Absalom

So the people went out into the field against Israel and the battle was in the wood of Ephraim, where the people of Israel were slain before the servants of David, and there was there a great slaughter that day of twenty thousand men For the battle was there scattered over the face of all the country and the wood devoured more people that day than the sword devoured

And Absalom met the servants of David And Absalom rode upon a mule, and the mule went under the thick boughs of a great oak, and his head caught hold of the oak, and he was taken up between the heaven and the earth, and the mule that was under him went away

And a certain man saw it, and told Joab, and said, Behold I saw Absalom hanged in an oak

And Joab said unto the man that told him, And, behold, thou sawest him, and why didst thou not smite him there to the ground? and I would have given thee ten shekels of silver, and a girdle

And the man said unto Joab, Though I should receive a thousand shekels of silver in mine hand, yet would I not put forth mine hand against the king's son for in our hearing the king charged thee and Abishai and Ittai, saying, Beware that none touch the young man Absalom Otherwise I should have wrought falsehood against mine own life for there is no matter hid from the king, and thou thyself wouldst have set thyself against me

Then said Joab, I may not tarry thus with thee And he took three darts in his hand, and thrust them through the heart of Absalom, while he was yet alive in the midst of the oak And ten young men that bare Joab's armor compassed about and smote Absalom, and slew him And Joab blew the trumpet, and the people returned from pursuing after Israel for Joab held back the people And they took Absalom, and cast him into a great pit in the wood, and laid a very great heap of stones upon him and all Israel fled every one to his tent —*2 Samuel xviii, 1–17*

G. Doré

DAVID MOURNING OVER ABSALOM.

Then said Ahimaaz the son of Zadok, Let me now run, and bear the king tidings, how that the Lord hath avenged him of his enemies. And Joab said unto him, Thou shalt not bear tidings this day, but thou shalt bear tidings another day: but this day thou shalt bear no tidings, because the king's son is dead. Then said Joab to Cushi, Go tell the king what thou hast seen. And Cushi bowed himself unto Joab, and ran. Then said Ahimaaz the son of Zadok yet again to Joab, But howsoever, let me, I pray thee, also run after Cushi. And Joab said, Wherefore wilt thou run, my son, seeing that thou hast no tidings ready? But howsoever, said he let me run. And he said unto him, Run. Then Ahimaaz ran by the way of the plain, and overran Cushi.

And David sat between the two gates: and the watchman went up to the roof over the gate unto the wall, and lifted up his eyes, and looked, and behold a man running alone. And the watchman cried, and told the king. And the king said, If he be alone, there is tidings in his mouth. And he came apace, and drew near. And the watchman saw another man running: and the watchman called unto the porter, and said, Behold another man running alone. And the king said, He also bringeth tidings. And the watchman said, Me thinketh the running of the foremost is like the running of Ahimaaz the son of Zadok. And the king said, He is a good man, and cometh with good tidings.

And Ahimaaz called, and said unto the king, All is well. And he fell down to the earth upon his face before the king, and said, Blessed be the Lord thy God, which hath delivereth up the men that lifted up their hand against my lord the king. And the king said, Is the young man Absalom safe? And Ahimaaz answered, When Joab sent the king's servant, and me thy servant, I saw a great tumult, but I knew not what it was. And the king said unto him, Turn aside, and stand here. And he turned aside, and stood still.

And, behold, Cushi came; and Cushi said, Tidings, my lord the king: for the Lord hath avenged thee this day of all them that rose up against thee. And the king said unto Cushi, Is the young man Absalom safe? And Cushi answered, The enemies of my lord the king, and all that rise against thee to do thee hurt, be as that young man is.

And the king was much moved, and went up to the chamber over the gate, and wept: and as he went, thus he said, O my son Absalom, my son, my son Absalom! would God I had died for thee, O Absalom, my son, my son!

And it was told Joab, Behold the king weepeth and mourneth for Absalom. And the victory that day was turned into mourning unto all the people: for the people heard say that day how the king was grieved for his son. And the people gat them by stealth that day into the city, as people being ashamed steal away when they flee in battle.

But the king covered his face, and the king cried with a loud voice, O my son Absalom, O Absalom, my son, my son!—*2 Samuel xviii, 19–33; xix, 1–4.*

SOLOMON.

And David took him more concubines and wives out of Jerusalem, after he was come from Hebron: and there were yet sons and daughters born to David. And these be the names of those that were born unto him in Jerusalem; Shammuah, and Shobab, and Nathan, and Solomon, Ibhar also, and Elishua, and Nepheg, and Japhia, and Elishama, and Eliada, and Eliphalet.—*2 Samuel v, 13–16.*

And David comforted Bath-sheba his wife, and went in unto her, and lay with her: and she bare a son, and he called his name Solomon: and the Lord loved him.—*2 Samuel xii, 24.*

So David slept with his fathers, and was buried in the city of David. And the days that David reigned over Israel were forty years: seven years reigned he in Hebron, and thirty and three years reigned he in Jerusalem.

Then sat Solomon upon the throne of David his father, and his kingdom was established greatly.—*1 Kings ii, 10–12.*

And God gave Solomon wisdom and understanding exceeding much, and largeness of heart, even as the sand that is on the sea shore. And Solomon's wisdom excelled the wisdom of all the children of the east country, and all the wisdom of Egypt. For he was wiser than all men; than Ethan the Ezrahite, and Heman, and Chalcol, and Darda, the sons of Mahol: and his fame was in all nations round about. And he spake three thousand proverbs: and his songs were a thousand and five. And he spake of trees, from the cedar tree that is in Lebanon even unto the hyssop that springeth out of the wall: he spake also of beasts, and of fowl, and of creeping things, and of fishes. And there came of all people to hear the wisdom of Solomon, from all kings of the earth, which had heard of his wisdom.—*2 Kings iv, 29–34.*

THE JUDGMENT OF SOLOMON.

Then came there two women, that were harlots, unto the king, and stood before him.

And the one woman said, O my lord, I and this woman dwell in one house; and I was delivered of a child with her in the house. And it came to pass the third day after that I was delivered, that this woman was delivered also: and we were together; there was no stranger with us in the house, save we two in the house. And this woman's child died in the night; because she overlaid it. And she arose at midnight, and took my son from beside me, while thine handmaid slept, and laid it in her bosom, and laid her dead child in my bosom. And when I rose in the morning to give my child suck, behold, it was dead: but when I had considered it in the morning, behold, it was not my son, which I did bear.

And the other woman said, Nay; but the living is my son, and the dead is thy son.

And this said, No; but the dead is thy son, and the living is my son.

Thus they spake before the king.

Then said the king, The one saith, This is my son that liveth, and thy son is the dead: and the other saith, Nay; but thy son is the dead, and my son is the living. And the king said, Bring me a sword.

And they brought a sword before the king.

And the king said, Divide the living child in two, and give half to the one, and half to the other.

Then spake the woman whose the living child was unto the king, for her bowels yearned upon her son, and she said, O my lord, give her the living child, and in no wise slay it.

But the other said, Let it be neither mine nor thine, but divide it.

Then the king answered and said, Give her the living child, and in no wise slay it: she is the mother thereof.

And all Israel heard of the judgment which the king had judged; and they feared the king: for they saw that the wisdom of God was in him, to do judgment. — *1 Kings iii, 16–28.*

THE CÉDARS DESTINED FOR THE TEMPLE.

And Hiram king of Tyre sent his servants unto Solomon; for he had heard that they had nointed him king in the room of his father: for Hiram was ever a lover of David.

And Solomon sent to Hiram, saying, Thou knowest how that David my father could not uild a house unto the name of the Lord his God for the wars which were about him on every de, until the Lord put them under the soles of his feet. But now the Lord my God hath ven me rest on every side, so that there is neither adversary nor evil occurrent. And, behold, purpose to build a house unto the name of the Lord my God, as the Lord spake unto avid my father, saying, Thy son, whom I will set upon thy throne in thy room, he shall build house unto my name. Now therefore command thou that they hew me cedar trees out of ebanon; and my servants shall be with thy servants: and unto thee will I give hire for thy rvants according to all that thou shalt appoint: for thou knowest that there is not among us ny that can skill to hew timber like unto the Sidonians.

And it came to pass, when Hiram heard the words of Solomon, that he rejoiced greatly, nd said, Blessed be the Lord this day, which hath given unto David a wise son over this great eople. And Hiram sent to Solomon, saying, I have considered the things which thou sentest me for: and I will do all thy desire concerning timber of cedar, and concerning timber of fir. ly servants shall bring them down from Lebanon unto the sea; and I will convey them by a in floats unto the place that thou shalt appoint me, and will cause them to be discharged ere, and thou shalt receive them: and thou shalt accomplish my desire, in giving food for my ousehold.

So Hiram gave Solomon cedar trees and fir trees according to all his desire.

And Solomon gave Hiram twenty thousand measures of wheat for food to his household, nd twenty measures of pure oil: thus gave Solomon to Hiram year by year.

And the Lord gave Solomon wisdom, as he promised him: and there was peace between iram and Solomon; and they two made a league together.

And king Solomon raised a levy out of all Israel; and the levy was thirty thousand men. nd he sent them to Lebanon, ten thousand a month by courses: a month they were in Leba-on, and two months at home: and Adoniram was over the levy. And Solomon had three-ore and ten thousand that bare burdens, and fourscore thousand hewers in the mountains; eside the chief of Solomon's officers which were over the work, three thousand and three undred, which ruled over the people that wrought in the work. And the king commanded, nd they brought great stones, costly stones, and hewed stones, to lay the foundation of the ouse. And Solomon's builders, and Hiram's builders did hew them, and the stone-squarers: they prepared timber and stones to build the house.—*1 Kings v.*

BARBANT

THE PROPHET SLAIN BY A LION.

Now there dwelt an old prophet in Bethel; and his sons came and told him all the 'orks that the man of God had done that day in Bethel: the words which he had spoken nto the king, them they told also to their father. And their father said unto them, Vhat way went he? For his sons had seen what way the man of God went, which came 'om Judah. And he said unto his sons, Saddle me the ass. So they saddled him the ss: and he rode thereon, and went after the man of God, and found him sitting under n oak: and he said unto him, Art thou the man of God that camest from Judah? And e said, I am. Then he said unto him, Come home with me, and eat bread. And he aid, I may not return with thee, nor go in with thee: neither will I eat bread nor drink 'ater with thee in this place: for it was said to me by the word of the Lord, Thou halt eat no bread nor drink water there, nor turn again to go by the way that thou amest. He said unto him, I am a prophet also as thou art; and an angel spake unto me y the word of the Lord, saying, Bring him back with thee into thine house, that he may at bread and drink water. But he lied unto him. So he went back with him, and did at bread in his house, and drank water.

And it came to pass, as they sat at the table, that the word of the Lord came unto ie prophet that brought him back: and he cried unto the man of God that came from udah, saying, Thus saith the Lord, Forasmuch as thou hast disobeyed the mouth of the .ord, and hast not kept the commandment which the Lord thy God commanded thee, ut camest back, and hast eaten bread and drunk water in the place, of the which the .ord did say to thee, Eat no bread, and drink no water; thy carcass shall not come unto ie sepulchre of thy fathers.

And it came to pass, after he had eaten bread, and after he had drunk, that he iddled for him the ass, to wit, for the prophet whom he had brought back.

And when he was gone, a lion met him by the way, and slew him: and his carcass as cast in the way, and the ass stood by it, the lion also stood by the carcass.

And, behold, men passed by, and saw the carcass cast in the way, and the lion standig by the carcass: and they came and told it in the city where the old prophet dwelt. .nd when the prophet that brought him back from the way heard thereof, he said, It is ie man of God, who was disobedient unto the word of the Lord: therefore the Lord ath delivered him unto the lion, which hath torn him, and slain him, according to the ord of the Lord, which he spake unto him. And he spake to his sons, saying, Saddle ie the ass. And they saddled him.

And he went and found his carcass cast in the way, and the ass and the lion standing y the carcass: the lion had not eaten the carcass, nor torn the ass.—*1 Kings xiii, 11–28.*

ELIJAH DESTROYING THE MESSENGERS OF AHAZIAH.

And Ahaziah fell down through a lattice in his upper chamber that was in Samaria, and was sick: and he sent messengers, and said unto them, Go, enquire of Baal-zebub the god of Ekron whether I shall recover of this disease.

But the angel of the Lord said to Elijah the Tishbite, Arise, go up to meet the messengers of the king of Samaria, and say unto them, Is it not because there is not a God in Israel, that ye go to enquire of Baal-zebub the god of Ekron? Now therefore thus saith the Lord, Thou shalt not come down from that bed on which thou art gone up, but shalt surely die. And Elijah departed.

And when the messengers turned back unto him, he said unto them, Why are ye now turned back? And they said unto him, There came a man up to meet us, and said unto us, Go, turn again unto the king that sent you, and say unto him, Thus saith the Lord, Is it not because there is not a God in Israel, that thou sendest to enquire of Baal-zebub the god of Ekron? therefore thou shalt not come down from that bed on which thou art gone up, but shalt surely die. And he said unto them, What manner of man was he which came up to meet you, and told you these words? And they answered him, He was an hairy man, and girt with a girdle of leather about his loins. And he said, It is Elijah the Tishbite.

Then the king sent unto him a captain of fifty with his fifty. And he went up to him: and, behold, he sat on the top of an hill. And he spake unto him, Thou man of God, the king hath said, Come down. And Elijah answered and said to the captain of fifty, If I be a man of God, then let fire come down from heaven, and consume thee and thy fifty. And there came down fire from heaven and consumed him and his fifty.

Again also he sent unto him another captain of fifty with his fifty. And he answered and said unto him, O man of God, thus hath the king said, Come down quickly. And Elijah answered and said unto them, If I be a man of God, let fire come down from heaven, and consume thee and thy fifty. And the fire of God came down from heaven and consumed him and his fifty.

And he sent again a captain of the third fifty with his fifty. And the third captain of fifty went up, and came and fell on his knees before Elijah, and besought him, and said unto him, O man of God, I pray thee, let my life, and the life of these fifty thy servants, be precious in thy sight. Behold, there came fire down from heaven, and burnt up the two captains of the former fifties with their fifties: therefore let my life now be precious in thy sight.

And the angel of the lord said unto Elijah, Go down with him: be not afraid of him. And he arose, and went down with him unto the king. And he said unto him, Thus saith the Lord, Forasmuch as thou hast sent messengers to enquire of Baal-zebub the god of Ekron, is it not because there is no God in Israel to enquire of his word? therefore thou shalt not come down off that bed on which thou art gone up, but shalt surely die.

So he died according to the word of the Lord which Elijah had spoken.—*2 Kings i, 2–17.*

ELIJAH'S ASCENT IN A CHARIOT OF FIRE.

And it came to pass, when the Lord would take up Elijah into heaven by a whirlwind, that Elijah went with Elisha from Gilgal. And Elijah said unto Elisha, Tarry here, I pray thee; for the Lord hath sent me to Beth-el. And Elisha said unto him, As the Lord liveth, and as thy soul liveth, I will not leave thee. So they went down to Beth-el.

And the sons of the prophets that were at Beth-el came forth to Elisha, and said unto him, Knowest thou that the Lord will take away thy master from thy head to-day? And he said, Yea, I know it; hold ye your peace. And Elijah said unto him, Elisha, tarry here, I pray thee; for the Lord hath sent me to Jericho. And he said, As the Lord liveth, and as thy soul liveth, I will not leave thee. So they came to Jericho.

And the sons of the prophets that were at Jericho came to Elisha, and said unto him, Knowest thou that the Lord will take away thy master from thy head to-day? And he answered, Yea, I know it; hold ye your peace. And Elijah said unto him, Tarry, I pray thee, here; for the Lord hath sent me to Jordan. And he said, As the Lord liveth, and as thy soul liveth, I will not leave thee. And they two went on.

And fifty men of the sons of the prophets went, and stood to view afar off: and they two stood by Jordan.

And Elijah took his mantle, and wrapped it together, and smote the waters, and they were divided hither and thither, so that they two went over on dry ground.

And it came to pass, when they were gone over, that Elijah said unto Elisha, Ask what I shall do for thee, before I be taken away from thee. And Elisha said, I pray thee, let a double portion of thy spirit be upon me. And he said, Thou hast asked a hard thing: nevertheless, if thou see me when I am taken from thee, it shall be so unto thee; but if not, it shall not be so.

And it came to pass, as they still went on, and talked, that, behold, there appeared a chariot of fire, and horses of fire, and parted them both asunder; and Elijah went up by a whirlwind into heaven.—*2 Kings ii, 1–11.*

THE DEATH OF JEZEBEL.

And when Jehu was come to Jezreel, Jezebel heard of it; and she painted her face, and tired her head, and looked out at a window. And as Jehu entered in at the gate, she said, Had Zimri peace, who slew his master?

And he lifted up his face to the window, and said, Who is on my side? who? And there looked out to him two or three eunuchs. And he said, Throw her down. So they threw her down: and some of her blood was sprinkled on the wall, and on the horses: and he trod her under foot. And when he was come in, he did eat and drink, and said, Go, see now this cursed woman, and bury her: for she is a king's daughter. And they went to bury her: but they found no more of her than the scull, and the feet, and the palms of her hands. Wherefore they came again, and told him. And he said, This is the word of the Lord, which he spake by his servant Elijah the Tishbite, saying, In the portion of Jezreel shall dogs eat the flesh of Jezebel: and the carcass of Jezebel shall be as dung upon the face of the field in the portion of Jezreel; so that they shall not say, This is Jezebel.—*2 Kings ix, 30-37.*

ESTHER CONFOUNDING HAMAN.

So the king and Haman came to banquet with Esther-the queen.

And the king said again unto Esther on the second day at the banquet of wine, What is thy petition, queen Esther? and it shall be granted thee: and what is thy request? and it shall be performed, even to the half of the kingdom.

Then Esther the queen answered and said, If I have found favor in thy sight, O king, and if it please the king, let my life be given me at my petition, and my people at my request: for we are sold, I and my people, to be destroyed, to be slain, and to perish. But if we had been sold for bondmen and bondwomen, I had held my tongue, although the enemy could not countervail the king's damage.

Then the king Ahasuerus answered and said unto Esther the queen, Who is he, and where is he, that durst presume in his heart to do so?

And Esther said, The adversary and enemy is this wicked Haman.

Then Haman was afraid before the king and the queen. And the king arising from the banquet of wine in his wrath went into the palace garden: and Haman stood up to make request for his life to Esther the queen; for he saw that there was evil determined against him by the king.

Then the king returned out of the palace garden into the place of the banquet of wine; and Haman was fallen upon the bed whereon Esther was. Then said the king, Will he force the queen also before me in the house?

As the word went out of the king's mouth, they covered Haman's face. And Harbonah, one of the chamberlains, said before the king, Behold also, the gallows fifty cubits high, which Haman had made for Mordecai, who had spoken good for the king, standeth in the house of Haman. Then the king said, Hang him thereon.

So they hanged Haman on the gallows that he had prepared for Mordecai. Then was the king's wrath pacified.—*Esther vii.*

ISAIAH

Isaiah (in Hebrew, *Yeshayahu*, "Salvation of God"), the earliest and most sublime of the four greater Hebrew prophets, was the son of Amoz (2 Kings xix, 2–20, Isaiah xxxvii, 2), and he uttered his oracles during the reigns of Uzziah, Jotham, Ahaz, and Hezekiah, kings of Judah The dates of his birth and death are unknown, but he lived from about 760 B C. to about 700 B C He was married and had three sons—the children referred to in Isaiah viii, 18, and he appears to have resided near Jerusalem

But by most competent critics it is now held that the last twenty-seven chapters (40–66) of the book bearing his name were the work, not of the prophet, but of a later writer who is commonly styled the second or Deutero-Isaiah In this portion of the book, Cyrus, who was not born till after 600 B C, is mentioned by name (Isaiah, xliv, 28 xlv, 1), and events which did not take place till a century after the prophet's death are referred to as happening contemporaneously with the writer's account of them The style of these last twenty-seven chapters, also, is different, and the tone is more elevated and spiritual

Dore's ideal portrait is more suited to the second or pseudo-Isaiah, than to the real one

DESTRUCTION OF SENNACHERIB'S HOST.

Therefore thus saith the Lord concerning the king of Assyria, He shall not come into this city, nor shoot an arrow there, nor come before it with shield, nor cast a bank against it. By the way that he came, by the same shall he return, and shall not come into this city, saith the Lord. For I will defend this city, to save it, for mine own sake, and for my servant David's sake.

And it came to pass that night that the angel of the Lord went out, and smote in the camp of the Assyrians an hundred fourscore and five thousand: and when they arose early in the morning, behold, they were all dead corpses.

So Sennacherib king of Assyria departed, and went and returned, and dwelt at Nineveh. And it came to pass, as he was worshipping in the house of Nisroch his god, that Adrammelech and Sharezer his sons smote him with the sword: and they escaped into the land of Armenia. And Esar-haddon his son reigned in his stead.—*2 Kings xix, 32–37.*

BARUCH

And it came to pass in the fourth year of Jehoiakim the son of Josiah king of Judah, that this word came unto Jeremiah from the Lord, saying, Take thee a roll of a book, and write therein all the words that I have spoken unto thee against Israel, and against Judah, and against all the nations, from the day I spake unto thee, from the days of Josiah, even unto this day It may be that the house of Judah will hear all the evil which I purpose to do unto them, that they may return every man from his evil way, that I may forgive their iniquity and their sin

Then Jeremiah called Baruch the son of Neriah and Baruch wrote from the mouth of Jeremiah all the words of the Lord, which he had spoken unto him, upon a roll of a book—*Jeremiah xxxvi, 1–4*

The word that Jeremiah the prophet spake unto Baruch the son of Neriah, when he had written these words in a book at the mouth of Jeremiah, in the fourth year of Jehoiakim the son of Josiah king of Judah, saying, Thus saith the Lord, the God of Israel, unto thee, O Baruch, thou didst say, Woe is me now! for the Lord hath added grief to my sorrow, I fainted in my sighing, and I find no rest

Thus shalt thou say unto him, The Lord saith thus, Behold, that which I have built will I break down, and that which I have planted I will pluck up, even this whole land And seekest thou great things for thyself? seek them not for, behold, I will bring evil upon all flesh, saith the Lord but thy life will I give unto thee for a prey in all places whither thou goest.—*Jeremiah xlv, 1–5*

EZEKIEL PROPHESYING

Ezekiel, the third of the great Hebrew prophets, was the son of the priest Buzi (Ezekiel i, 3) He was probably born about 620 or 630 years before Christ, and was consequently a contemporary of Jeremiah and Daniel, to the latter of whom he alludes in chapters xiv, 14–20 and xxviii, 3 When Jerusalem was taken by Nebuchadnezzar in 597 B C (2 Kings xxiv, 8–16, Jeremiah xxix, 1–2, Ezekiel xvii, 12, xix, 9), Ezekiel was carried captive along with Jehoiachin, or Jeconiah, king of Judah, and thousands of other Jewish prisoners, to Babylonia, or as he himself calls it, "the land of the Chaldeans" (Ezekiel i, 3) Here, along with his exiled fellow-countrymen, he lived on the banks of the river Chebar (Ezekiel i, 1–3), in a house of his own (viii, 1) Here also he married, and here, too, his wife, "the desire of his eyes," was taken from him "with a stroke" (Ezekiel xxiv, 15–18) His prophetic career extended over twenty-two years, from about 592 B C to about 570 B C.

The book bearing his name is written in a mystical and symbolical style, and abounds with visions and difficult allegories which indicate on the part of the author the possession of a vivid and sublime imagination Ezekiel's authorship of it has been questioned The Talmud attributes it to the Great Synagogue, of which Ezekiel was not a member It is divisible into two portions The first (chapters i–xxiv) was written before, and the second (chapters xxv–xlviii) after, the destruction of Jerusalem by Nebuchadnezzar in 586 B C, the eleventh year of the prophet's captivity (Ezekiel xxvi, 1–2, xl, 1) The present text is very imperfect, being corrupted by the interpolation of glosses and other additions by later hands.

Dore's picture represents the prophet uttering his oracles to his fellow-exiles ("them of the captivity"), or to the "elders of Judah," or "elders of Israel," on one of the occasions to which he himself alludes (viii, 1, xi, 25, xiv, 1, xx, 1).

G. Doré

THE VISION OF EZEKIEL.

The hand of the Lord was upon me, and carried me out in the Spirit of the Lord, and set me down in the midst of the valley which was full of bones, and caused me to pass by them round about: and, behold, there were very many in the open valley; and, lo, they were very dry.

And he said unto me, Son of man, can these bones live?

And I answered, O Lord God, thou knowest.

Again he said unto me, Prophesy upon these bones, and say unto them, O ye dry bones, hear the word of the Lord. Thus saith the Lord God unto these bones; Behold, I will cause breath to enter into you, and ye shall live: And I will lay sinews upon you, and will bring up flesh upon you, and cover you with skin, and put breath in you, and ye shall live; and ye shall know that I am the Lord.

So I prophesied as I was commanded: and as I prophesied, there was a noise, and behold a shaking, and the bones came together, bone to his bone. And when I beheld, lo, the sinews and the flesh came up upon them, and the skin covered them above: but there was no breath in them.

Then said he unto me, Prophesy unto the wind, prophesy, son of man, and say to the wind, Thus saith the Lord God; Come from the four winds, O breath, and breathe upon these slain, that they may live.

So I prophesied as he commanded me, and the breath came into them, and they lived, and stood up upon their feet, an exceeding great army.

Then he said unto me, Son of man, these bones are the whole house of Israel: behold, they say, Our bones are dried, and our hope is lost: we are cut off for our parts. Therefore prophesy and say unto them, Thus saith the Lord God; Behold, O my people, I will open your graves, and cause you to come up out of your graves, and bring you into the land of Israel. And ye shall know that I am the Lord, when I have opened your graves, O my people, and brought you up out of your graves, and shall put my Spirit in you, and ye shall live, and I shall place you in your own land: then shall ye know that I the Lord have spoken it, and performed it, saith the Lord.—*Ezekiel xxxvii, 1–14.*

DANIEL

Respecting the parentage or family of Daniel, the fourth of the great Hebrew prophets, nothing is known, though he appears to have been of noble if not of royal descent (Daniel i, 3) When, in the third year of the reign of King Jehoiakim (607, 606, 605, or 604 B C), Jerusalem was first taken by Nebuchadnezzar, Daniel, then a youth, was among the captives carried to Babylon By the king's orders, he, with others of the Jewish youth, was educated for three years (Daniel i, 3–7) At this time Daniel acquired the power of interpreting dreams (i, 17), which he used with such advantage in expounding a dream of Nebuchadnezzar, that he was made ruler over the whole province of Babylon (Daniel ii, 46–48). Daniel's interpretation of Belshazzar's famous vision having been fulfilled by the capture of Babylon by Darius, that conqueror promoted Daniel to the highest office in the kingdom (Daniel vi, 1–3) The prophet also prospered greatly during the reign of Cyrus (Daniel vi, 28)

The book of Daniel is written partly in Chaldaic or Syriac (the vernacular Aramaic language spoken by the people of Palestine), and partly in sacred Hebrew. It is manifestly divisible into two portions The first (chapters i–vi) narrating the details of the prophet's life, and the second (chapters vii–xii) setting forth his apocalyptic visions. Much doubt has been cast upon the authenticity of the work. The evident reference in the eleventh chapter to the conquest of Persia by Alexander the Great, which took place about 330 B C., or more than two hundred years after Daniel flourished, has led many modern critics to believe that the work was composed in the time of the Maccabees

Dore's picture appears to be intended to represent the prophet meditating over one of the many visions which came to him.

THE FIERY FURNACE.

Wherefore at that time certain Chaldeans came near, and accused the Jews. They spake and said to the king Nebuchadnezzar, O king, live forever. There are certain Jews whom thou hast set over the affairs of the province of Babylon, Shadrach, Meshach, and Abed-nego; these men, O king, have not regarded thee: they serve not thy gods, nor worship the golden image which thou hast set up.

Then Nebuchadnezzar in his rage and fury commanded to bring Shadrach, Meshach, and Abed-nego. Then they brought these men before the king.

Nebuchadnezzar spake and said unto them, Is it true, O Shadrach, Meshach, and Abed-nego? do not ye serve my gods, nor worship the golden image which I have set up? Now if ye be ready that at what time ye hear the sound of the cornet, flute, harp, sackbut, psaltery, and dulcimer, and all kinds of music, ye fall down and worship the image which I have made; well: but if ye worship not, ye shall be cast the same hour into the midst of a burning fiery furnace; and who is that God that shall deliver you out of my hands?

Shadrach, Meshach, and Abed-nego, answered and said to the king, O Nebuchadnezzar, we are not careful to answer thee in this matter. If it be so, our God whom we serve is able to deliver us from the burning fiery furnace, and he will deliver us out of thine hand, O king. But if not, be it known unto thee, O king, that we will not serve thy gods, nor worship the golden image which thou hast set up.

Then was Nebuchadnezzar full of fury, and the form of his visage was changed against Shadrach, Meshach, and Abed-nego: therefore he spake, and commanded that they should heat the furnace one seven times more than it was wont to be heated. And he commanded the most mighty men that were in his army to bind Shadrach, Meshach, and Abed-nego, and to cast them into the burning fiery furnace.

Then these men were bound in their coats, their hosen, and their hats, and their other garments, and were cast into the midst of the burning fiery furnace. Therefore because the king's commandment was urgent, and the furnace exceeding hot, the flame of the fire slew those men that took up Shadrach, Meshach, and Abed-nego. And these three men, Shadrach, Meshach, and Abed-nego fell down bound into the midst of the burning fiery furnace.

Then Nebuchadnezzar the king was astonished, and rose up in haste, and spake, and said unto his counselors, Did not we cast three men bound into the midst of the fire?

They answered, and said unto the king, True, O king.

He answered and said, Lo, I see four men loose, walking in the midst of the fire, and they have no hurt; and the form of the fourth is like the Son of God.

Then Nebuchadnezzar came near to the mouth of the burning fiery furnace, and spake, and said, Shadrach, Meshach, and Abed-nego, ye servants of the most high God, come forth and come hither. Then Shadrach, Meshach, aud Abed-nego, came forth of the midst of the fire. And the princes, governors, and captains, and the king's counselors, being gathered together, saw these men, upon whose bodies the fire had no power, nor was a hair of their head singed, neither were their coats changed, nor the smell of fire had passed on them.—*Daniel iii, 8, 9, 12–27.*

BELSHAZZAR'S FEAST.

Belshazzar the king made a great feast to a thousand of his lords, and drank wine before the thousand. Belshazzar, whiles he tasted the wine, commanded to bring the golden and silver vessels which his father Nebuchadnezzar had taken out of the temple which was in Jerusalem; that the king, and his princes, his wives, and his concubines, might drink therein. Then they brought the golden vessels that were taken out of the temple of the house of God which was at Jerusalem; and the king, and his princes, his wives, and his concubines, drank in them. They drank wine and praised the gods of gold, and of silver, of brass, of iron, of wood, and of stone.

In the same hour came forth fingers of a man's hand, and wrote over against the candlestick upon the plaister of the wall of the king's palace: and the king saw the part of the hand that wrote. Then the king's countenance was changed, and his thoughts troubled him, so that the joints of his loins were loosed, and his knees smote one against another.

[On the failure of his astrologers and soothsayers to interpret the writing, the king, at the suggestion of his queen, sends for Daniel, who interprets it as follows:]

O thou king, the most high God gave Nebuchadnezzar thy father a kingdom, and majesty, and glory, and honor: and for the majesty that he gave him, all peoples, nations, and languages, trembled and feared before him: whom he would he slew; and whom he would he kept alive; and whom he would he set up; and whom he would he put down. But when his heart was lifted up, and his mind hardened in pride, he was deposed from his kingly throne, and they took his glory from him: and he was driven from the sons of men; and his heart was made like the beasts, and his dwelling was with the wild asses: they fed him with grass like oxen, and his body was wet with the dew of heaven; till he knew that the most high God ruled in the kingdom of men, and that he appointeth over it whomsoever he will.

And thou his son, O Belshazzar, hast not humbled thine heart, though thou knewest all this; but hast lifted up thyself against the Lord of heaven; and they have brought the vessels of his house before thee, and thou, and thy lords, thy wives, and thy concubines, have drunk wine in them; and thou hast praised the gods of silver, and gold, of brass, iron, wood, and stone, which see not, nor hear, nor know: and the God in whose hand thy breath is, and whose are all thy ways, hast thou not glorified:

Then was the part of the hand sent from him; and this writing was written.

And this is the writing that was written, MENE, MENE, TEKEL, UPHARSIN. This is the interpretation of the thing: MENE; God hath numbered thy kingdom and finished it. TEKEL; Thou art weighed in the balances, and art found wanting. PERES; Thy kingdom is divided, and given to the Medes and Persians.

In that night was Belshazzar the king of the Chaldeans slain. And Darius the Median took the kingdom.—*Daniel v.*

DANIEL IN THE LIONS' DEN.

Now when Daniel knew that the writing was signed, he went into his house; and his windows being open in his chamber toward Jerusalem, he kneeled upon his knees three times a day, and prayed, and gave thanks before his God, as he did aforetime.

Then these men assembled, and found Daniel praying and making supplication before his God. Then they came near, and spake before the king concerning the king's decree; Hast thou not signed a decree, that every man that shall ask a petition of any God or man within thirty days, save of thee, O king, shall be cast into the den of lions.

The king answered and said, The thing is true, according to the law of the Medes and Persians, which altereth not.

Then answered they and said before the king, That Daniel, which is of the children of the captivity of Judah, regardeth not thee, O king, nor the decree that thou hast signed, but maketh his petition three times a day.

Then the king, when he heard these words, was sore displeased with himself, and set his heart on Daniel to deliver him: and he laboured till the going down of the sun to deliver him.

Then these men assembled unto the king, and said unto the king, Know, O king, that the law of the Medes and Persians is, That no decree nor statute which the king establisheth may be changed. Then the king commanded, and they brought Daniel and cast him into the den of lions. Now the king spake and said unto Daniel, Thy God whom thou servest continually, he will deliver thee. And a stone was brought, and laid upon the mouth of the den; and the king sealed it with his own signet, and with the signet of his lords; that the purpose might not be changed concerning Daniel.

Then the king went to his palace, and passed the night fasting: neither were instruments of musick brought before him: and his sleep went from him. Then the king arose very early in the morning, and went in haste unto the den of lions. And when he came to the den, he cried with a lamentable voice unto Daniel: and the king spake and said to Daniel, O Daniel, servant of the living God, is thy God, whom thou servest continually, able to deliver thee from the lions?

Then said Daniel unto the King, O king, live forever. My God hath sent his angel, and hath shut the lions' mouths, that they have not hurt me: forasmuch as before him innocency was found in me; and also before thee, O king, have I done no hurt.

Then was the king exceeding glad for him, and commanded that they should take Daniel up out of the den. So Daniel was taken up out of the den, and no manner of hurt was found upon him, because he believed in his God. And the king commanded, and they brought those men which had accused Daniel, and they cast them into the den of lions, them, their children, and their wives; and the lions had the mastery of them, and brake all their bones in pieces or ever they came at the bottom of the den.—*Daniel vi, 10–24.*

THE PROPHET AMOS

Amos, one of the earliest of the Hebrew prophets, flourished during the reign of Uzziah, about 790 B C, and was consequently a contemporary of Hosea and Joel In his youth he lived at Tekoa, about six miles south of Bethlehem, in Judæa, and was a herdsman and a gatherer of sycamore fruit (Amos i, 1, vii, 14) This occupation he gave up for that of prophet (vii, 15), and he came forward to denounce the idolatry then prevalent in Judah, Israel, and the surrounding kingdoms

The first six chapters of his book contain his denunciations of idolatry, the other three, his symbolical vision of the overthrow of the people of Israel, and a promise of their restoration The style is remarkable for clearness and strength, and for its picturesque use of images drawn from the rural and pastoral life which the prophet had led in his youth

JONAH CALLING NINEVEH TO REPENTANCE

And the word of the Lord came unto Jonah the second time, saying, Arise, go unto Nineveh, that great city, and preach unto it the preaching that I bid thee.

So Jonah arose, and went unto Nineveh, according to the word of the Lord Now Nineveh was an exceeding great city of three days' journey And Jonah began to enter into the city a day's journey, and he cried, and said, Yet forty days, and Nineveh shall be overthrown.

So the people of Nineveh believed God, and proclaimed a fast, and put on sackcloth, from the greatest of them even to the least of them For word came unto the king of Nineveh, and he arose from his throne, and he laid his robe from him, and covered him with sackcloth, and sat in ashes And he caused it to be proclaimed and published through Nineveh by the decree of the king and his nobles, saying, Let neither man nor beast, herd nor flock taste anything let them not feed, nor drink water: but let man and beast be covered with sackcloth, and cry mightily unto God yea, let them turn every one from his evil way, and from the violence that is in their hands Who can tell if God will turn and repent, and turn away from his fierce anger, that we perish not?

And God saw their works, that they turned from their evil way, and God repented of the evil, that he had said that he would do unto them; and he did it not —*Jonah iii*

DANIEL CONFOUNDING THE PRIESTS OF BEL

Now the Babylonians had an idol called Bel and there were spent upon him every day twelve great measures of fine flour, and forty sheep, and sixty vessels of wine. The king also worshipped him, and went every day to adore him but Daniel adored his God And the king said unto him. Why dost thou not adore Bel? And he answered, and said to him Because I do not worship idols made with hands, but the living God, that created heaven and earth, and hath power over all flesh. And the king said to him. Doth not Bel seem to thee to be a living God? Seest thou not how much he eateth and drinketh every day? Then Daniel smiled and said. O king, be not deceived: for this is but clay within, and brass without, neither hath he eaten at any time

And the king being angry called for his priests, and said to them If you tell me not, who it is that eateth up these expenses, you shall die But if you can show that Bel eateth these things, Daniel shall die, because he hath blasphemed against Bel

And Daniel said to the king. Be it done according to thy word

Now the priests of Bel were seventy besides their wives and little ones and children. And they went with Daniel into the temple of Bel And the priests of Bel said: Behold, we go out· and do thou, O king, set on the meats, and make ready, the wine, and shut the door fast, and seal it with thy own ring. and when thou comest in the morning, if thou findest not that Bel hath eaten all up, we will suffer death, or else Daniel that hath lied against us

And they little regarded it, because they had made under the table a secret entrance, and they always came in by it, and consumed those things

So it came to pass after they were gone out, the king set the meats before Bel and Daniel commanded his servants, and they brought ashes, and he sifted them all over the temple before the king. and going forth they shut the door, and having sealed it with the king's ring, they departed

But the priests went in by night, according to their custom, with their wives and their children: and they eat and drank all up

And the king rose early in the morning, and Daniel with him And the king said· Are the seals whole, Daniel? and he answered. They are whole, O king And as soon as he had opened the door, the king looked upon the table, and cried out with a loud voice Great art thou, O Bel, and there is not any deceit with thee And Daniel laughed· and he held the king that he should not go in and he said Behold the pavement, mark whose footsteps these are. And the king said: I see the footsteps of men, and women, and children And the king was angry Then he took the priests, and their wives, and their children and they showed him the private doors by which they came in, and consumed the things that were on the table

The king therefore put them to death, and delivered Bel into the power of Daniel. who destroyed him, and his temple.—*Daniel xiv, 1–21 (Douay Version).*

HELIODORUS PUNISHED IN THE TEMPLE.

But Heliodorus executed that which he had resolved on, himself being present in the same place with his guard about the treasury

But the spirit of the Almighty God gave a great evidence of his presence, so that all that had presumed to obey him, falling down by the power of God, were struck with fainting and dread For there appeared to them a horse with a terrible rider upon him, adorned with a very rich covering and he ran fiercely and struck Heliodorus with his fore-feet, and he that sat upon him seemed to have armor of gold Moreover, there appeared two other young men, beautiful and strong, bright and glorious, and in comely apparel who stood by him, on either side, and scourged him without ceasing with many stripes

And Heliodorus suddenly fell to the ground, and they took him up covered with great darkness, and having put him into a litter they carried him out So he that came with many servants, and all his guard into the aforesaid treasury, was carried out, no one being able to help him, the manifest power of God being known And he indeed by the power of God lay speechless, and without all hope of recovery.—*2 Maccabees iii, 23–29*

THE NATIVITY

And it came to pass in those days, that there went out a decree from Cæsar Augustus, that all the world should be taxed (And this taxing was first made when Cyrenius was governor of Syria) And all went to be taxed, every one into his own city

And Joseph also went up from Galilee, out of the city of Nazareth, into Judæa, unto the city of David, which is called Bethlehem, (because he was of the house and lineage of David) to be taxed with Mary, his espoused wife, being great with child And so it was, that, while they were there, the days were accomplished that she should be delivered And she brought forth her firstborn son, and wrapped him in swaddling clothes, and laid him in a manger, because there was no room for them in the inn.

And there were in the same country shepherds abiding in the field, keeping watch over their flock by night And, lo, the angel of the Lord came upon them, and the glory of the Lord shone round about them and they were sore afraid And the angel said unto them, Fear not: for, behold, I bring you good tidings of great joy, which shall be to all people For unto you is born this day in the city of David a Saviour, which is Christ the Lord. And this shall be a sign unto you; Ye shall find the babe wrapped in swaddling clothes, lying in a manger And suddenly there was with the angel a multitude of the heavenly host praising God, and saying, Glory to God in the highest, and on earth peace, good will toward men

And it came to pass, as the angels were gone away from them into heaven, the shepherds said one to another, Let us now go even unto Bethlehem, and see this thing which is come to pass, which the Lord hath made known unto us And they came with haste, and found Mary, and Joseph, and the babe lying in a manger. And when they had seen it, they made known abroad the saying which was told them concerning this child And all they that heard it, wondered at those things which were told them by the shepherds But Mary kept all these things, and pondered them in her heart And the shepherds returned, glorifying and praising God for all the things that they had heard and seen, as it was told unto them

And when eight days were accomplished for the circumcising of the child, his name was called Jesus, which was so named of the angel before he was conceived in the womb.—*Luke ii, 1–21*

THE STAR IN THE EAST.

Now when Jesus was born in Bethlehem of Judæa in the days of Herod the king, behold, there came wise men from the east to Jerusalem, saying, Where is he that is born King of the Jews? for we have seen his star in the east, and are come to worship him

When Herod the king had heard these things, he was troubled, and all Jerusalem with him And when he had gathered all the chief priests and scribes of the people together, he demanded of them where Christ should be born And they said unto him, In Bethlehem of Judæa. for thus it is written by the prophet, And thou Bethlehem, in the land of Juda, are not the least among the princes of Juda for out of thee shall come a Governor, that shall rule my people Israel

Then Herod, when he had privily called the wise men, enquired of them diligently what time the star appeared And he sent them to Bethlehem, and said, Go and search diligently for the young child, and when ye have found him, bring me word again, that I may come and worship him also. When they had heard the king, they departed; and, lo, the star, which they saw in the east, went before them, till it came and stood over where the young child was When they saw the star, they rejoiced with exceeding great joy.—*Matthew ii, 1–10.*

THE FLIGHT INTO EGYPT

And when they were departed, behold, the angel of the Lord appeareth to Joseph in a dream, saying, Arise, and take the young child and his mother, and flee into Egypt, and be thou there until I bring thee word for Herod will seek the young child to destroy him

When he arose, he took the young child and his mother by night, and departed into Egypt · and was there until the death of Herod that it might be fulfilled which was spoken of the Lord by the prophet, saying, Out of Egypt have I called my son —*Matthew ii, 13–15.*

THE MASSACRE OF THE INNOCENTS

Then Herod, when he saw that he was mocked of the wise men, was exceeding wroth, and sent forth, and slew all the children that were in Bethlehem, and in all the coasts thereof, from two years old and under, according to the time which he had diligently enquired of the wise men

Then was fulfilled that which was spoken by Jeremy the prophet, saying, In Rama was there a voice heard, lamentation, and weeping, and great mourning, Rachel weeping for her children, and would not be comforted, because they are not.—*Matthew ii, 16–18*

JESUS QUESTIONING THE DOCTORS.

Now his parents went to Jerusalem every year at the feast of the passover.

And when he was twelve years old, they went up to Jerusalem after the custom of the feast. And when they had fulfilled the days, as they returned, the child Jesus tarried behind in Jerusalem; and Joseph and his mother knew not of it. But they, supposing him to have been in the company, went a day's journey; and they sought him among their kinsfolk and acquaintance. And when they found him not, they turned back again to Jerusalem, seeking him.

And it came to pass, that after three days they found him in the temple, sitting in the midst of the doctors, both hearing them, and asking them questions. And all that heard him were astonished at his understanding and answers.

And when they saw him, they were amazed: and his mother said unto him, Son, why hast thou thus dealt with us? behold, thy father and I have sought thee sorrowing. And he said unto them, How is it that ye sought me? wist ye not that I must be about my father's business? And they understood not the saying which he spake unto them.

And he went down with them, and came to Nazareth, and was subject unto them: but his mother kept all these sayings in her heart.

And Jesus increased in wisdom and stature, and in favor with God and man.—*Luke ii, 41–52.*

JESUS HEALING THE SICK

And Jesus went about all Galilee, teaching in their synagogues, and preaching the gospel of the kingdom, and healing all manner of sickness and all manner of disease among the people And his fame went throughout all Syria · and they brought unto him all sick people that were taken with divers diseases and torments, and those which were possessed with devils, and those which were lunatic, and those that had the palsy, and he healed them —*Matthew iv, 23–24*

SERMON ON THE MOUNT.

And there followed him great multitudes of people from Galilee, and from Decapolis, and from Jerusalem, and from Judæa, and from beyond Jordan.

And seeing the multitudes, he went up into a mountain: and when he was set, his disciples came unto him. And he opened his mouth and taught them.

*   *   *   *   *   *   *   *

And it came to pass, when Jesus had ended these sayings, the people were astonished at his doctrine: For he taught them as one having authority, and not as the scribes.

When he was come down from the mountain, great multitudes followed him.—*Matthew iv, 25; v, 1–2, 28–29; viii, 1.*

CHRIST STILLING THE TEMPEST.

And when he was entered into a ship, his disciples followed him. And, behold, there arose a great tempest in the sea, insomuch that the ship was covered with the waves: but he was asleep. And his disciples came to him, and awoke him, saying, Lord, save us: we perish. And he saith unto them, Why are ye fearful, O ye of little faith? Then he arose, and rebuked the winds and the sea; and there was a great calm. But the men marveled, saying, What manner of man is this, that even the winds and the sea obey him?—*Matthew viii, 23–27.*

THE DUMB MAN POSSESSED.

As they went out, behold, they brought to him a dumb man possessed with a devil. And when the devil was cast out, the dumb spake: and the multitudes marveled, saying, It was never so seen in Israel.

But the Pharisees said, He casteth out devils through the prince of the devils.—*Matthew ix, 32–34.*

CHRIST IN THE SYNAGOGUE.

And it came to pass, that when Jesus had finished these parables, he departed thence. And when he was come into his own country, he taught them in their synagogue, insomuch that they were astonished, and said, Whence hath this man this wisdom, and these mighty works? Is not this the carpenter's son? is not his mother called Mary? and his brethren, James, and Joses, and Simon, and Judas? And his sisters, are they not all with us? Whence then hath this man all these things?

And they were offended in him. But Jesus said unto them, A prophet is not without honor, save in his own country, and in his own house.

And he did not many mighty works there because of their unbelief.—*Matthew xiii, 53–58.*

THE DISCIPLES PLUCKING CORN ON THE SABBATH.

And it came to pass, that he went through the corn fields on the sabbath day; and his disciples began, as they went, to pluck the ears of corn.

And the Pharisees said unto him, Behold, why do they on the sabbath day that which is not lawful?

And he said unto them, Have ye never read what David did, when he had need, and was an hungered, he, and they that were with him? How he went into the house of God in the days of Abiathar the high priest, and did eat the shewbread, which is not lawful to eat but for the priest, and gave also to them which were with him? And he said unto them, The sabbath was made for man, and not man for the sabbath: Therefore the Son of man is Lord also of the sabbath.—*Mark ii, 23-28.*

JESUS WALKING ON THE WATER.

And when he had sent them away, he departed into a mountain to pray. And when even was come, the ship was in the midst of the sea, and he alone on the land. And he saw them toiling in rowing; for the wind was contrary unto them: and about the fourth watch of the night he cometh unto them, walking upon the sea, and would have passed by them. But when they saw him walking upon the sea, they supposed it had been a spirit, and cried out: for they all saw him, and were troubled. And immediately he talked with them, and saith unto them, Be of good cheer: it is I; be not afraid.

And he went up unto them into the ship; and the wind ceased: and they were sore amazed in themselves beyond measure, and wondered. For they considered not the miracle of the loaves; for their heart was hardened.—*Mark vi, 46–52.*

G. Doré
H. PISAN

CHRIST'S ENTRY INTO JERUSALEM.

And when they drew nigh unto Jerusalem, and were come to Bethphage, unto the mount of Olives, then sent Jesus two disciples, saying unto them, Go into the village over against you, and straightway ye shall find an ass tied, and a colt with her: loose them, and bring them unto me. And if any man say ought unto you, ye shall say, The Lord hath need of them; and straightway he will send them.

All this was done that it might be fulfilled which was spoken by the prophet, saying, Tell ye the daughter of Sion, Behold, thy King cometh unto thee, meek, and sitting upon an ass, and a colt the foal of an ass.

And the disciples went, and did as Jesus commanded them, and brought the ass, and the colt, and put on them their clothes, and they set him thereon.

And a very great multitude spread their garments in the way; others cut down branches from the trees, and strewed them in the way. And the multitudes that went before, and that followed, cried, saying, Hosanna to the son of David: Blessed is he that cometh in the name of the Lord; Hosanna in the highest.

And when he was come into Jerusalem, all the city was moved, saying, Who is this? And the multitude said, This is Jesus the prophet of Nazareth of Galilee.—*Matthew xxi, 1–11.*

JESUS AND THE TRIBUTE MONEY.

And they send unto him certain of the Pharisees and of the Herodians, to catch him in his words.

And when they were come, they say unto him, Master, we know that thou art true, and carest for no man: for thou regardest not the person of men, but teachest the way of God in truth: Is it lawful to give tribute to Cæsar, or not? Shall we give, or shall we not give?

But he, knowing their hypocrisy, said unto them, Why tempt ye me? bring me a penny, that I may see it. And they brought it.

And he saith unto them, Whose is this image and superscription?

And they said unto him, Cæsar's.

And Jesus answering said unto them, Render to Cæsar the things that are Cæsar's, and to God the things that are God's.

And they marveled at him.—*Mark xii, 13–17.*

THE WIDOW'S MITE.

And Jesus sat over against the treasury, and beheld how the people cast money into the treasury: and manyethat were rich cast in much.

And there came a certain poor widow, and she threw in two mites, which make a farthing. And he called unto him his disciples, and saith unto them, Verily I say unto you, That this poor widow hath cast more in, than all they which have cast into the treasury: for all they did cast in of their abundance; but she of her want did cast in all that she had, even all her living.—*Mark xii, 41–44.*

RAISING OF THE DAUGHTER OF JAIRUS.

And, behold, there cometh one of the rulers of the synagogue, Jairus by name; and when he saw him, he fell at his feet, and besought him greatly, saying, My little daughter lieth at the point of death: I pray thee, come and lay thy hands on her, that she may be healed; and she shall live. And Jesus went with him; and much people followed him, and thronged him.

And a certain woman which had an issue of blood twelve years, and had suffered many things of many physicians, and had spent all that she had, and was nothing bettered, but rather grew worse, when she had heard of Jesus, came in the press behind, and touched his garment. For she said, If I may touch but his clothes, I shall be whole. And straightway the fountain of her blood was dried up; and she felt in her body that she was healed of that plague. And Jesus, immediately knowing in himself that virtue had gone out of him, turned him about in the press, and said, Who touched my clothes? And his disciples said unto him, Thou seest the multitude thronging thee, and sayest thou, Who touched me? And he looked round about to see her that had done this thing. But the woman fearing and trembling, knowing what was done in her, came and fell down before him, and told him all the truth. And he said unto her Daughter, thy faith hath made the whole; go in peace, and be whole of thy plague.

While he yet spake, there came from the ruler of the synagogue's house certain which said, Thy daughter is dead: why troublest thou the Master any further? As soon as Jesus heard the word that was spoken, he saith unto the ruler of the synagogue, Be not afraid, only believe. And he suffered no man to follow him, save Peter, and James, and John the brother of James. And he cometh to the house of the ruler of the synagogue, and seeth the tumult, and them that wept and wailed greatly. And when he was come in, he saith unto them, Why make ye this ado, and weep? the damsel is not dead, but sleepeth. And they laughed him to scorn. But when he had put them all out, he taketh the father and the mother of the damsel, and them that were with him, and entereth in where the damsel was lying. And he took the damsel by the hand, and said unto her, Talitha cumi; which is, being interpreted, Damsel, I say unto thee, arise. And straightway the damsel arose, and walked; for she was of the age of twelve years. And they were astonished with a great astonishment.

And he charged them straitly that no man should know it; and commanded that something should be given her to eat.—*Mark v, 22–43.*

THE GOOD SAMARITAN.

But he, willing to justify himself, said unto Jesus, And who is my neighbor?

And Jesus answering said, A certain man went down from Jerusalem to Jericho, and fell among thieves, which stripped him of his raiment, and wounded him, and departed, leaving him half dead. And by chance there came down a certain priest that way: and when he saw him, he passed by on the other side. And likewise a Levite, when he was at the place, came and looked on him, and passed by on the other side. But a certain Samaritan, as he journeyed, came where he was: and when he saw him, he had compassion on him. And went to him, and bound up his wounds, pouring in oil and wine, and set him on his own beast, and brought him to an inn, and took care of him. And on the morrow when he departed, he took out two pence, and gave them to the host, and said unto him, Take care of him; and whatsoever thou spendest more, when I come again, I will repay thee. Which now of these three, thinkest thou, was neighbor unto him that fell among the thieves?

And he said, He that shewed mercy on him.

Then said Jesus unto him, Go, and do thou likewise.—*Luke x, 29–37.*

ARRIVAL OF THE SAMARITAN AT THE INN.

But a certain Samaritan, as he journeyed, came where he was; and when he saw him, he had compassion on him, and went to him, and bound up his wounds, pouring in oil and wine, and set him on his own beast, and brought him to an inn, and took care of him.—*Luke x, 33–34.*

THE PRODIGAL SON.

Likewise, I say unto you, there is joy in the presence of the angels of God over one sinner that repenteth.

And he said, a certain man had two sons: and the younger of them said to his father, Father, give me the portion of goods that falleth to me. And he divided unto them his living.

And not many days after the younger son gathered all together, and took his journey into a far country, and there wasted his substance with riotous living. And when he had spent all, there arose a mighty famine in that land; and he began to be in want. And he went and joined himself to a citizen of that country; and he sent him into his fields to feed swine. And he would fain have filled his belly with the husks that the swine did eat: and no man gave unto him.

And when he came to himself, he said, How many hired servants of my father's have bread enough and to spare, and I perish with hunger! I will arise and go to my father, and will say unto him, Father, I have sinned against heaven, and before thee, and am no more worthy to be called thy son: make me as one of thy hired servants.

And he arose, and came to his father. But when he was yet a great way off, his father saw him, and had compassion, and ran, and fell on his neck, and kissed him. And the son said unto him, Father, I have sinned against heaven, and in thy sight, and am no more worthy to be called thy son. But the father said to his servants, Bring forth the best robe, and put it on him; and put a ring on his hand, and shoes on his feet: And bring hither the fatted calf, and kill it; and let us eat, and be merry: for this my son was dead, and is alive again; he was lost, and is found. And they began to be merry.

Now his elder son was in the field: and as he came and drew nigh to the house, he heard music and dancing. And he called one of the servants, and asked what these things meant.

And he said unto him, thy brother is come; and thy father hath killed the fatted calf, because he hath received him safe and sound.

And he was angry, and would not go in: therefore came his father out, and intreated him. And he answering said to his father, Lo, these many years do I serve thee, neither transgressed I at any time thy commandment: and yet thou never gavest me a kid, that I might make merry with my friends: but as soon as this thy son was come, which hath devoured thy living with harlots, thou hast killed for him the fatted calf.

And he said unto him, Son, thou art ever with me, and all that I have is thine. It was meet that we should make merry, and be glad: for this thy brother was dead, and is alive again; and was lost, and is found.—*Luke xv, 10–32.*

LAZARUS AND THE RICH MAN.

There was a certain rich man, which was clothed in purple and fine linen, and fared sumptuously every day:

And there was a certain beggar named Lazarus, which was laid at his gate, full of sores, and desiring to be fed with the crumbs which fell from the rich man's table: moreover the dogs came and licked his sores.

And it came to pass, that the beggar died, and was carried by the angels into Abraham's bosom: the rich man also died, and was buried; and in hell he lifted up his eyes, being in torments, and seeth Abraham afar off, and Lazarus in his bosom. And he cried and said, Father Abraham, have mercy on me, and send Lazarus, that he may dip the tip of his finger in water and cool my tongue; for I am tormented in this flame.

But Abraham said, Son, remember that thou in thy lifetime receivedst thy good things, and likewise Lazarus evil things: but now he is comforted, and thou art tormented. And beside all this, between us and you there is a great gulf fixed: so that they which would pass from hence to you cannot; neither can they pass to us, that would come from thence.

Then he said, I pray thee therefore, father, that thou wouldest send him to my father's house: for I have five brethren; that he may testify unto them, lest they also come into this place of torment.

Abraham saith unto him, They have Moses and the prophets; let them hear them.

And he said, Nay, father Abraham: but if one went unto them from the dead, they will repent.

And he said unto him, If they hear not Moses and the prophets, neither will they be persuaded, though one rose from the dead.—*Luke xvi, 19–31.*

THE PHARISEE AND THE PUBLICAN.

And he spake this parable unto certain which trusted in themselves that they were righteous, and despised others:

Two men went up into the temple to pray; the one a Pharisee, and the other a publican. The Pharisee stood and prayed thus with himself, God, I thank thee, that I am not as other men are, extortioners, unjust, adulterers, or even as this publican. I fast twice in the week, I give tithes of all that I possess. And the publican, standing afar off, would not lift up so much as his eyes unto heaven, but smote upon his breast, saying, God be merciful to me a sinner. I tell you, this man went down to his house justified rather than the other: for every one that exalteth himself shall be abased; and he that humbleth himself shall be exalted.—*Luke xviii, 9–14.*

JESUS AND THE WOMAN OF SAMARIA.

Then cometh he to a city of Samaria, which is called Sychar, near to the parcel of ground that Jacob gave to his son Joseph. Now Jacob's well was there. Jesus therefore, being wearied with his journey, sat thus on the well: and it was about the sixth hour. There cometh a woman of Samaria to draw water: Jesus saith unto her, Give me to drink.

(For his disciples were gone away unto the city to buy meat.)

Then saith the woman of Samaria unto him, How is it that thou, being a Jew, askest drink of me, which am a woman of Samaria? for the Jews have no dealings with the Samaritans.

Jesus answered and said unto her, If thou knewest the gift of God, and who it is that saith to thee, Give me to drink; thou wouldest have asked of him, and he would have given thee living water.

The woman saith unto him, Sir, thou hast nothing to draw with, and the well is deep: from whence then hast thou that living water? Art thou greater than our father Jacob, which gave us the well, and drank thereof himself, and his children, and his cattle?

Jesus answered and said unto her, Whosoever drinketh of this water shall thirst again: but whosoever drinketh of the water that I shall give him shall never thirst; but the water that I shall give him shall be in him a well of water springing up into everlasting life.

The woman saith unto him, Sir, give me this water, that I thirst not, neither come hither to draw.

Jesus saith unto her, Go, call thy husband, and come hither.

The woman answered and said, I have no husband.

Jesus said unto her, Thou hast well said, I have no husband: for thou hast had five husbands; and he whom thou now hast is not thy husband: in that saidst thou truly.

The woman saith unto him, Sir, I perceive that thou art a prophet. Our fathers worshiped in this mountain; and ye say, that in Jerusalem is the place where men ought to worship.

Jesus saith unto her, Woman, believe me, the hour cometh, when ye shall neither in this mountain, nor yet at Jerusalem, worship the Father. Ye worship ye know not what: we know what we worship; for salvation is of the Jews. But the hour cometh, and now is, when the true worshipers shall worship the Father in spirit and in truth: for the Father seeketh such to worship him. God is a Spirit: and they that worship him must worship him in spirit and in truth.

The woman saith unto him, I know that Messias cometh, which is called Christ: when he is come, he will tell us all things.

Jesus saith unto her, I that speak unto thee am he.

And upon this came his disciples, and marveled that he talked with the woman: yet no man said, What seekest thou? or, Why talkest thou with her?

The woman then left her waterpot, and went her way into the city, and saith to the men, Come, see a man, which told me all things, that ever I did: is not this the Christ?

Then they went out of the city, and came unto him.—*John iv, 5–30.*

JESUS AND THE WOMAN TAKEN IN ADULTERY.

Jesus went unto the mount of Olives. And early in the morning he came again into the temple, and all the people came unto him; and he sat down, and taught them.

And the scribes and Pharisees brought unto him a woman taken in adultery; and when they had set her in the midst, they say unto him, Master, this woman was taken in adultery, in the very act. Now Moses in the law commanded us, that such should be stoned: but what sayest thou? This they said, tempting him, that they might have to accuse him.

But Jesus stooped down, and with his finger wrote on the ground, as though he heard them not.

So when they continued asking him, he lifted up himself, and said unto them, He that is without sin among you, let him first cast a stone at her.

And again he stooped down, and wrote on the ground.

And they which heard it, being convicted by their own conscience, went out one by one, beginning at the eldest, even unto the last; and Jesus was left alone, and the woman standing in the midst.

When Jesus had lifted up himself, and saw none but the woman, he said unto her, Woman where are those thine accusers? hath no man condemned thee?

She said, No man, Lord.

And Jesus said unto her, Neither do I condemn thee: go, and sin no more.—*John viii, 1–11.*

THE RESURRECTION OF LAZARUS.

Now Jesus was not yet come into the town, but was in that place where Martha met him. The Jews then which were with her in the house, and comforted her, when they saw Mary, that she rose up hastily and went out, followed her, saying, She goeth unto the grave to weep there. Then when Mary was come where Jesus was, and saw him, she fell down at his feet, saying unto him, Lord, if thou hadst been here, my brother had not died.

When Jesus therefore saw her weeping, and the Jews also weeping which came with her, he groaned in the spirit, and was troubled, and said, Where have ye laid him?

They said unto him, Lord, come and see.

Jesus wept.

Then said the Jews, Behold how he loved him! And some of them said, Could not this man, which opened the eyes of the blind, have caused that even this man should not have died?

Jesus therefore again groaning in himself cometh to the grave. It was a cave and a stone lay upon it. Jesus said, Take ye away the stone.

Martha, the sister of him that was dead, saith unto him, Lord, by this time he stinketh: for he hath been dead four days.

Jesus saith unto her, Said I not unto thee, that, if thou wouldest believe, thou shouldest see the glory of God?

Then they took away the stone from the place where the dead was laid.

And Jesus lifted up his eyes, and said, Father, I thank thee that thou hast heard me. And I knew that thou hearest me always: but because of the people which stand by I said it, that they may believe that thou hast sent me.

And when he thus had spoken, he cried with a loud voice, Lazarus, come forth.

And he that was dead came forth, bound hand and foot with graveclothes: and his face was bound about with a napkin.

Jesus saith unto them, Loose him, and let him go.

Then many of the Jews which came to Mary, and had seen the things which Jesus did, believed on him.—*John xi, 30–45.*

MARY MAGDALENE.

Of Mary "called Magdalene" (Luke viii, 2) but few particulars are recorded in scripture. We first hear of her as having been delivered by Jesus of seven devils (Luke viii, 1–3; Mark xvi, 9). Impelled, no doubt, by gratitude for her deliverance, she becomes one of his followers, accompanying him thenceforward in all his wanderings faithfully till his death. She was the first person to whom he appeared after his resurrection (Mark xvi, 9; John xx, 1, 11–18). The common belief that she was a fallen woman is destitute of the slightest foundation. On the contrary, the references to her as being in the company of such women as Joanna, the wife of Herod's steward, Salome, the mother of James and John, and Mary, the mother of Jesus (Luke viii, 3; Mark xvi, 40; John xix, 25), strongly discountenance such a supposition. The error, which had no other source than ecclesiastical tradition, has been fostered and perpetuated by the stupid blunder of the translators of the authorized version in identifying her with the "sinner" who is described in Luke vii, 37–50 as washing the feet of Jesus with her tears (see head-note to Luke vii).

The Roman Catholic notion that this "sinner" was Mary the sister of Lazarus is almost equally groundless (see Douay Bible, head-note to Matthew xxvi, and the foot-note references to Luke vii, 37, found in most Catholic Bibles). The only reason for this identification is that the anointing by the "sinner" is described as taking place in the house of a Pharisee named Simon (Luke vii, 36, 39–40, 43–44); that the anointing by the unnamed woman, as described in Matthew xxvi, 6–13 and Mark xiv, 3–9, took place in the house of one "Simon the leper," in Bethany; and that Mary, the sister of Lazarus, is described in John xi, 2, and xii, 3–8, as anointing Jesus in a house (apparently that of Lazarus himself) in Bethany, when a conversation ensues altogether different from that recorded in Luke vii, but similar to that related in Matthew xxvi, and Mark xiv, save that the objection to the anointing of Jesus is made, not by "his disciples" (Matthew xxvi, 8), not by "some that had indignation" (Mark xiv, 4), but by "one of his disciples, Judas Iscariot, Simon's son" (John xii, 4). The demeanor of Mary, the sister of Lazarus, is, however, by no means that of a fallen and sinful though penitent woman, but that of a pious and good one (see Luke x, 39, 42; John xi, 28–33; xii, 3).

Dore's illustration, which portrays Mary Magdalene as a heartbroken and despairing sinner, shows that he has fallen into the common error.

G. Doré

THE LAST SUPPER.

Now the first day of the feast of unleavened bread the disciples came to Jesus, saying unto him, Where wilt thou that we prepare for thee to eat the passover? And he said, Go into the city to such a man, and say unto him, The Master saith, My time is at hand; I will keep the passover at thy house with my disciples. And the disciples did as Jesus had appointed them; and they made ready the passover.

Now when the even was come, he sat down with the twelve. And as they did eat, he said, Verily I say unto you, that one of you shall betray me.

And they were exceeding sorrowful, and began every one of them to say unto him, Lord, is it I?

And he answered and said, He that dippeth his hand with me in the dish, the same shall betray me. The Son of man goeth as it is written of him: but woe unto that man by whom the Son of man is betrayed! it had been good for that man if he had not been born.

Then Judas, which betrayed him, answered and said, Master, is it I?

He said unto him, Thou hast said.

And as they were eating, Jesus took bread, and blessed it, and brake it, and gave it to the disciples, and said, Take, eat; this is my body. And he took the cup, and gave thanks, and gave it to them, saying, Drink ye all of it; for this is my blood of the new testament, which is shed for many for the remission of sins. But I say unto you, I will not drink henceforth of this fruit of the vine, until that day when I drink it new with you in my Father's kingdom.

And when they had sung an hymn, they went out into the mount of Olives.—*Matthew xxvi, 17–30.*

G. Doré

THE AGONY IN THE GARDEN.

And he came out, and went, as he was wont, to the mount of Olives; and his discip.es also followed him. And when he was at the place, he said unto them, Pray that ye enter not into temptation.

And he was withdrawn from them about a stone's cast, and kneeled down, and prayed. Saying, Father, if thou be willing, remove this cup from me: nevertheless not my will, but thine, be done.

And there appeared an angel unto him from heaven, strengthening him.

And being in an agony he prayed more earnestly: and his sweat was as it were great drops of blood falling down to the ground.

And when he rose up from prayer, and was come to his disciples, he found them sleeping for sorrow, and said unto them, Why sleep ye? rise and pray, lest ye enter into temptation. —*Luke xxii, 39–46.*

PRAYER OF JESUS IN THE GARDEN OF OLIVES.

Then cometh Jesus with them unto a place called Gethsemane, and saith unto the disciples, Sit ye here, while I go and pray yonder. And he took with him Peter and the two sons of Zebedee, and began to be sorrowful and very heavy. Then saith he unto them, My soul is exceeding sorrowful, even unto death: tarry ye here, and watch with me.

And he went a little farther, and fell on his face, and prayed, saying, O my Father, if it be possible, let this cup pass from me: nevertheless not as I will, but as thou wilt.

And he cometh unto the disciples, and findeth them asleep, and saith unto Peter, What, could ye not watch with me one hour? Watch and pray, that ye enter not into temptation: the spirit indeed is willing, but the flesh is weak.

He went away again the second time, and prayed, saying, O my Father, if this cup may not pass away from me, except I drink it, thy will be done.

And he came and found them asleep again: for their eyes were heavy.

And he left them, and went away again, and prayed the third time, saying the same words.

Then cometh he to his disciples, and saith unto them, Sleep on now, and take your rest: behold, the hour is at hand, and the Son of man is betrayed into the hands of sinners. Rise, let us be going: behold, he is at hand that doth betray me.—*Matthew xxvi, 36–46.*

THE BETRAYAL.

And he cometh the third time, and saith unto them, Sleep on now, and take your rest: it is enough, the hour is come; behold, the Son of man is betrayed into the hands of sinners. Rise up, let us go; lo, he that betrayeth me is at hand.

And immediately, while he yet spake, cometh Judas, one of the twelve, and with him a great multitude with swords and staves, from the chief priests and the scribes and the elders. And he that betrayed him had given them a token, saying, Whomsoever I shall kiss, that same is he; take him, and lead him away safely. And as soon as he was come, he goeth straightway to him, and saith, Master, master; and kissed him.

And they laid their hands on him, and took him. And one of them that stood by drew a sword, and smote a servant of the high priest, and cut off his ear. And Jesus answered and said unto them, Are ye come out, as against a thief, with swords and with staves to take me? I was daily with you in the temple teaching, and ye took me not: but the scriptures must be fulfilled.

And they all forsook him, and fled.—*Mark xiv, 41–50.*

G. Doré

CHRIST FAINTING UNDER THE CROSS.

The incident depicted in this illustration seems to be as apocryphal as that embodied in the artist's picture of Mary Magdalene. There is absolutely no warrant in scripture for the notion that Christ fainted under the burden of the cross. The only foundation for such an idea to be found in the Bible is contained in the head note to Mark xv, which is quite unwarranted by the text. According to the three synoptic gospels the cross was borne not by Christ, but by Simon, a Cyrenian (see Matthew xxvii, 32; Mark xv, 21; Luke xxiii, 26). According to the fourth evangelist, Jesus bore the cross without assistance the whole distance to the place of crucifixion (John xix, 16–18). In not one of the four narratives is there so much as a hint that he fainted under the burden.

THE FLAGELLATION.

Then released he Barabbas unto them: and when he had scourged Jesus, he delivered him to be crucified.—*Matthew xxvii, 26.*

And so Pilate, willing to content the people, released Barabbas unto them, and delivered Jesus, when he had scourged him, to be crucified.—*Mark xv, 15.*

Then Pilate therefore took Jesus, and scourged him.—*John xix, 1.*

THE CRUCIFIXION.

And when they were come unto a place called Golgotha, that is to say, a place of a skull, they gave him vinegar to drink mingled with gall: and when he had tasted thereof, he would not drink. And they crucified him, and parted his garments, casting lots: that it might be fulfilled which was spoken by the prophet, They parted my garments among them, and upon my vesture did they cast lots. And sitting down they watched him there; and set up over his head his accusation written, THIS IS JESUS THE KING OF THE JEWS.

Then were there two thieves crucified with him, one on the right hand, and another on the left.

And they that passed by reviled him, wagging their heads, and saying, Thou that destroyest the temple, and buildest it in three days, save thyself. If thou be the Son of God, come down from the cross.

Likewise also the chief priests mocking him, with the scribes and elders, said, He saved others: himself he cannot save. If he be the King of Israel, let him now come down from the cross, and we will believe him. He trusted in God; let him deliver him now, if he will have him: for he said, I am the Son of God.

The thieves also, which were crucified with him, cast the same in his teeth.—*Matthew xxvii, 33–44.*

H. PISAN.

CLOSE OF THE CRUCIFIXION

Now from the sixth hour there was darkness over all the land unto the ninth hour And about the ninth hour Jesus cried with a loud voice, saying, Eli, Eli, lama sabachthani? that is to say, My God, my God, why hast thou forsaken me?

Some of them that stood there, when they heard that, said, This man calleth for Elias And straightway one of them ran, and took a spunge, and filled it with vinegar, and put it on a reed, and gave him to drink The rest said, Let be, let us see whether Elias will come to save him

Jesus, when he had cried again with a loud voice, yielded up the ghost

And, behold, the veil of the temple was rent in twain from the top to the bottom, and the earth did quake, and the rocks rent, and the graves were opened, and many bodies of the saints which slept arose, and came out of the graves after his resurrection, and went into the holy city, and appeared unto many.

Now when the centurion, and they that were with him, watching Jesus, saw the earthquake, and those things that were done, they feared greatly, saying, Truly this was the Son of God

And many women were there beholding afar off, which followed Jesus from Galilee, ministering unto him, among which was Mary Magdalene, and Mary the mother of James and Joses, and the mother of Zebedee's children —*Matthew xxvii, 45–56.*

THE BURIAL OF JESUS.

When the even was come, there came a rich man of Arimathea, named Joseph, who also himself was Jesus' disciple: he went to Pilate, and begged the body of Jesus. Then Pilate commanded the body to be delivered. And when Joseph had taken the body, he wrapped it in a clean linen cloth, and laid it in his own new tomb, which he had hewn out in the rock: and he rolled a great stone to the door of the sepulchre, and departed.

And there was Mary Magdalene, and the other Mary, sitting over against the sepulchre.—*Matthew xxvii, 57–61.*

THE ANGEL AT THE SEPULCHRE.

In the end of the sabbath, as it began to dawn toward the first day of the week, came Mary Magdalene and the other Mary to see the sepulchre.

And, behold, there was a great earthquake: for the angel of the Lord descended from heaven, and came and rolled back the stone from the door, and sat upon it. His countenance was like lightning, and his raiment white as snow: and for fear of him the keepers did shake, and became as dead men.

And the angel answered and said unto the women, Fear not ye: for I know that ye seek Jesus, which was crucified. He is not here: for he is risen, as he said. Come, see the place where the Lord lay. And go quickly, and tell his disciples that he is risen from the dead; and, behold, he goeth before you into Galilee; there shall ye see him: lo, I have told you.

And they departed quickly from the sepulchre with fear and great joy; and did run to bring his disciples word.—*Matthew xxviii, 1–8.*

G. Doré
H. PISAN

THE JOURNEY TO EMMAUS.

And, behold, two of them went that same day to a village called Emmaus which was from Jerusalem about threescore furlongs

And they talked together of all these things which had happened And it came to pass that, while they communed together and reasoned, Jesus himself drew near and went with them. But their eyes were holden that they should not know him

And he said unto them, What manner of communications are these that ye have one to another, as ye walk, and are sad?

And the one of them, whose name was Cleopas, answering said unto him, Art thou only a stranger in Jerusalem, and hast not known the things which are come to pass there in these days?

And he said unto them, What things?

And they said unto him, Concerning Jesus of Nazareth, which was a prophet mighty in deed and word before God and all the people · And how the chief priests and our rulers delivered him to be condemned to death, and have crucified him But we trusted that it had been he which should have redeemed Israel and beside all this, to-day is the third day since these things were done. Yea, and certain women also of our company made us astonished, which were early at the sepulchre, and when they found not his body, they came, saying, that they had also seen a vision of angels, which said that he was alive And certain of them which were with us went to the sepulchre, and found it even so as the women had said. but him they saw not

Then he said unto them, O fools, and slow of heart to believe all that the prophets have spoken. ought not Christ to have suffered these things, and to enter into his glory?

And beginning at Moses and all the prophets, he expounded unto them in all the scriptures the things concerning himself

And they drew nigh unto the village, whither they went. and he made as though he would have gone further But they constrained him, saying, Abide with us. for it is toward evening, and the day is far spent And he went in to tarry with them

And it came to pass, as he sat at meat with them, he took bread, and blessed it, and brake, and gave to them And their eyes were opened, and they knew him, and he vanished out of their sight

And they said one to another, Did not our heart burn within us, while he talked with us by the way, and while he opened to us the scriptures?

And they rose up the same hour, and returned to Jerusalem, and found the eleven gathered together, and them that were with them, saying, The Lord is risen indeed, and hath appeared to Simon.

And they told what things were done in the way, and how he was known of them in breaking of bread —*Luke xxiv, 13-35*

THE ASCENSION.

Now upon the first day of the week, very early in the morning, they came unto the sepulchre, bringing the spices which they had prepared, and certain others with them. And they found the stone rolled away from the sepulchre. * * *

And they remembered his words. And returned from the sepulchre, and told all these things unto the eleven, and to all the rest. * * *

And, behold, two of them went that same day to a village called Emmaus, which was from Jerusalem about threescore furlongs. And they talked together of all these things which had happened. * * *

And they rose up the same hour, and returned to Jerusalem, and found the eleven gathered together, and them that were with them, saying, The Lord is risen indeed, and hath appeared to Simon. And they told what things were done in the way, and how he was known of them in breaking of bread. And as they thus spake, Jesus himself stood in the midst of them, and saith unto them, Peace be unto you. * * *

And, behold, I send the promise of my Father upon you: but tarry ye in the city of Jerusalem, until ye be endued with power from on high.

And he led them out as far as to Bethany, and he lifted up his hands, and blessed them. And it came to pass, while he blessed them, he was parted from them, and carried up into heaven. And they worshiped him, and returned to Jerusalem with great joy.—*Luke xxiv, 1–2, 8–9, 13–14, 33–36, 49–52.*

The former treatise have I made, O Theophilus, of all that Jesus began both to do and teach, until the day in which he was taken up, after that he through the Holy Ghost had given commandments unto the apostles whom he had chosen: to whom also he shewed himself alive after his passion by many infallible proofs, being seen of them forty days, and speaking of the things pertaining to the kingdom of God: and, being assembled together with them, commanded them that they should not depart from Jerusalem, but wait for the promise of the Father, which, saith he, ye have heard of me. For John truly baptized with water; but ye shall be baptized with the Holy Ghost not many days hence.

When they therefore were come together, they asked of him, saying, Lord, wilt thou at this time restore again the kingdom of Israel? And he said unto them, It is not for you to know the times or the seasons, which the Father hath put in his own power. But ye shall receive power, after that the Holy Ghost is come upon you: and ye shall be witnesses unto me both in Jerusalem, and all Judæa, and in Samaria, and unto the uttermost part of the earth.

And when he had spoken these things, while they beheld, he was taken up: and a cloud received him out of their sight. And while they looked steadfastly toward heaven as he went up, behold, two men stood by them in white apparel.—*Acts i, 1–10.*

THE MARTYRDOM OF ST STEPHEN

And Stephen, full of faith and power, did great wonders and miracles among the people

Then there arose certain of the synagogue, which is called the synagogue of the Libertines, and Cyrenians, and Alexandrians, and of them of Cilicia and of Asia, disputing with Stephen. And they were not able to resist the wisdom and the spirit by which he spake Then they suborned men, which said, We have heard him speak blasphemous words against Moses and against God. And they stirred up the people, and the elders, and the scribes, and came upon him, and caught him, and brought him to the council And set up false witnesses, which said, This man ceaseth not to speak blasphemous words against this holy place, and the law for we have heard him say, that this Jesus of Nazareth shall destroy this place, and shall change the customs which Moses delivered us

And all that sat in the council, looking steadfastly on him, saw his face as it had been the face of an angel

Then said the high priest, Are these things so?

And he said, Men, brethren, and fathers, hearken [Stephen here makes his defense, concluding with a terrible denunciation of the Jews as being stiffnecked and persecutors of their prophets, and as betrayers and murderers of their latest one, Jesus Christ]

When they heard these things, they were cut to the heart, and they gnashed on him with their teeth

But he, being full of the Holy Ghost, looked up steadfastly into heaven, and saw the glory of God, and Jesus standing on the right hand of God, and said, Behold, I see the heavens opened, and the Son of man standing on the right hand of God

Then they cried out with a loud voice, and stopped their ears, and ran upon him with one accord, and cast him out of the city, and stoned him and the witnesses laid down their clothes at a young man's feet, whose name was Saul And they stoned Stephen, calling upon God, and saying, Lord Jesus, receive my spirit

And he kneeled down, and cried with a loud voice, Lord, lay not this sin to their charge. And when he had said this, he fell asleep

And Saul was consenting unto his death —*Acts vi, 8–15, vii, 1–2, 54–56, viii, 1*

G. Doré

SAUL'S CONVERSION.

And Saul, yet breathing out threatenings and slaughter against the disciples of the Lord, went unto the high priest, and desired of him letters to Damascus to the synagogues, that if he found any of this way, whether they were men or women, he might bring them bound unto Jerusalem.

And as he journeyed, he came near Damascus: and suddenly there shined round about him a light from heaven: and he fell to the earth, and heard a voice saying unto him, Saul, Saul, why persecutest thou me? And he said, Who art thou, Lord? And the Lord said, I am Jesus whom thou persecutest: it is hard for thee to kick against the pricks. And he trembling and astonished said, Lord, what wilt thou have me to do? And the Lord said unto him, Arise, and go into the city, and it shall be told thee what thou must do.

And the men which journeyed with him stood speechless, hearing a voice, but seeing no man.

And Saul arose from the earth; and when his eyes were opened, he saw no man: but they led him by the hand, and brought him into Damascus. And he was three days without sight, and neither did eat nor drink.

And there was a certain disciple at Damascus, named Ananias; and to him said the Lord in a vision, Ananias. And he said, Behold, I am here, Lord.

And the Lord said unto him, Arise, and go into the street which is called Straight, and enquire in the house of Judas for one called Saul, of Tarsus: for, behold, he prayeth, and hath seen in a vision a man named Ananias coming in, and putting his hand on him, that he might receive his sight. Then Ananias answered, Lord, I have heard by many of this man, how much evil he hath done to thy saints at Jerusalem: and here he hath authority from the chief priests to bind all that call on thy name. But the Lord said unto him, Go thy way: for he is a chosen vessel unto me, to bear my name before the Gentiles, and kings, and the children of Israel: for I will shew him how great things he must suffer for my name's sake.

And Ananias went his way, and entered into the house; and putting his hands on him said, Brother Saul, the Lord, even Jesus, that appeared unto thee in the way as thou camest, hath sent me, that thou mightest receive thy sight, and be filled with the Holy Ghost. And immediately there fell from his eyes as it had been scales: and he received sight forthwith, and arose and was baptized. And when he had received meat, he was strengthened.

Then was Saul certain days with the disciples which were at Damascus. And straightway he preached Christ in the synagogues, that he is the Son of God.—*Acts ix, 1–20.*

THE DELIVERANCE OF ST. PETER.

Now about that time Herod the king stretched forth his hands to vex certain of the church. And he killed James the brother of John with the sword.

And because he saw it pleased the Jews, he proceeded further to take Peter also. (Then were the days of unleavened bread.) And when he had apprehended him, he put him in prison, and delivered him to four quarternions of soldiers to keep him; intending after Easter to bring him forth to the people.

Peter therefore was kept in prison: but prayer was made without ceasing of the church unto God for him.

And when Herod would have brought him forth, the same night Peter was sleeping between two soldiers, bound with two chains: and the keepers before the door kept the prison. And, behold, the angel of the Lord came upon him, and a light shined in the prison: and he smote Peter on the side, and raised him up, saying, Arise up quickly. And his chains fell off from his hands. And the angel said unto him, Gird thyself, and bind on thy sandals: And so he did. And he saith unto him, Cast thy garment about thee, and follow me. And he went out, and followed him; and wist not that it was true which was done by the angel; but thought he saw a vision. When they were past the first and the second ward, they came unto the iron gate that leadeth unto the city; which opened to them of his own accord: and they went out and passed on through one street; and forthwith the angel departed from him.

And when Peter was come to himself, he said, Now I know of a surety, that the Lord hath sent his angel, and hath delivered me out of the hand of Herod, and from all the expectation of the people of the Jews.—*Acts xii, 1–11.*

PAUL AT EPHESUS.

And it came to pass, that, while Apollos was at Corinth, Paul having passed through the upper coasts came to Ephesus; and finding certain disciples, he said unto them, Have ye received the Holy Ghost since ye believed? And they said unto him, We have not so much as heard whether there be any Holy Ghost. And he said unto them, Unto what then were ye baptized? And they said, Unto John's baptism. Then said Paul, John verily baptized with the baptism of repentance, saying unto the people, that they should believe on him which should come after him, that is, on Christ Jesus.

When they heard this, they were baptized in the name of the Lord Jesus. And when Paul had laid his hands upon them, the Holy Ghost came on them; and they spake with tongues, and prophesied. And all the men were about twelve.

And he went into the synagogue, and spake boldly for the space of three months, disputing and persuading the things concerning the kingdom of God.

But when divers were hardened, and believed not, but spake evil of that way before the multitude, he departed from them, and separated the disciples, disputing daily in the school of one Tyrannus. And this continued by the space of two years; so that all they which dwelt in Asia heard the word of the Lord Jesus, both Jews and Greeks.

And God wrought special miracles by the hands of Paul: so that from his body were brought unto the sick handkerchiefs or aprons, and the diseases departed from them, and the evil spirits went out of them.

Then certain of the vagabond Jews, exorcists, took upon them to call over them which had evil spirits the name of the Lord Jesus, saying, We adjure you by Jesus whom Paul preacheth. And there were seven sons of one Sceva, a Jew, and chief of the priests, which did so. And the evil spirit answered and said, Jesus I know, and Paul I know; but who are ye? And the man in whom the evil spirit was leaped on them, and overcame them, and prevailed against them, so that they fled out of that house naked and wounded.

And this was known to all the Jews and Greeks also dwelling at Ephesus; and fear fell on them all, and the name of the Lord Jesus was magnified. And many that believed came, and confessed, and shewed their deeds. Many of them also which used curious arts brought their books together, and burned them before all men: and they counted the price of them, and found it fifty thousand pieces of silver.

So mightily grew the word of God and prevailed.—*Acts xix, 1-20.*

PAUL MENACED BY THE JEWS.

Do therefore this that we say to thee: We have four men which have a vow on them; them take, and purify thyself with them, and be at charges with them, that they may shave their heads: and all may know that those things, whereof they were informed concerning thee, are nothing; but that thou thyself also walkest orderly, and keepest the law. * * *

Then Paul took the men, and the next day purifying himself with them entered into the temple, to signify the accomplishment of the days of purification, until that an offering should be offered for every one of them.

And when the seven days were almost ended, the Jews which were of Asia, when they saw him in the temple, stirred up all the people, and laid hands on him, crying out, Men of Israel, help: this is the man, that teacheth all men every where against the people, and the law, and this place: and further brought Greeks also into the temple, and hath polluted this holy place. (For they had seen before with him in the city Trophimus an Ephesian, whom they supposed that Paul had brought into the temple.)

And all the city was moved, and the people ran together: and they took Paul, and drew him out of the temple: and forthwith the doors were shut. And as they went about to kill him, tidings came unto the chief captain of the band, that all Jerusalem was in an uproar: who immediately took soldiers and centurions, and ran down unto them: and when they saw the chief captain and the soldiers, they left beating of Paul. Then the chief captain came near, and took him, and commanded him to be bound with two chains; and demanded who he was, and what he had done. And some cried one thing, some another, among the multitude: and when he could not know the certainty for the tumult, he commanded him to be carried into the castle. And when he came upon the stairs, so it was, that he was borne of the soldiers for the violence of the people. For the multitude of the people followed after, crying, Away with him.

And as Paul was to be led into the castle, he said unto the chief captain, May I speak unto thee? Who said, Canst thou speak Greek? Art not thou that Egyptian, which before these days madest an uproar, and leddest out into the wilderness four thousand men that were murderers? But Paul said, I am a man which am a Jew of Tarsus, a city in Cilicia, a citizen of no mean city: and, I beseech thee, suffer me to speak unto the people.

And when he had given him license, Paul stood on the stairs, and beckoned with the hand unto the people. And when there was made a great silence, he spake unto them in the Hebrew tongue.—*Acts xxi, 23–40.*

PAUL'S SHIPWRECK.

And while the day was coming on, Paul besought them all to take meat, saying, This day is the fourteenth day that ye have tarried and continued fasting, having taken nothing. Wherefore I pray you to take some meat; for this is for your health: for there shall not a hair fall from the head of any of you.

And when he had thus spoken, he took bread, and gave thanks to God in presence of them all; and when he had broken it, he began to eat. Then were they all of good cheer, and they also took some meat.

And we were in all in the ship two hundred threescore and sixteen souls.

And when they had eaten enough, they lightened the ship, and cast out the wheat into the sea. And when it was day, they knew not the land: but they discovered a certain creek with a shore, into the which they were minded, if it were possible, to thrust in the ship. And when they had taken up the anchors, they committed themselves unto the sea, and loosed the rudder bands, and hoised up the mainsail to the wind, and made toward shore. And falling into a place where two seas met, they ran the ship aground; and the forepart stuck fast, and remained unmovable, but the hinder part was broken with the violence of the waves. And the soldiers' counsel was to kill the prisoners, lest any of them should swim out, and escape. But the centurion, willing to save Paul, kept them from their purpose; and commanded that they which could swim should cast themselves first into the sea, and get to land: and the rest, some on boards, and some on broken pieces of the ship. And so it came to pass, that they escaped all safe to land.

And when they were escaped, then they knew that the island was called Melita.

And the barbarous people shewed us no little kindness: for they kindled a fire, and received us every one, because of the present rain, and because of the cold.—*Acts xxvii, 33–44; xxviii, 1–2.*

DEATH ON THE PALE HORSE.

And when he had opened the fourth seal, I heard the voice of the fourth beast say, Come and see.

And I looked, and behold a pale horse: and his name that sat on him was Death, and Hell followed with him. And power was given unto them over the fourth part of the earth, to kill with sword, and with hunger, and with death, and with the beasts of the earth.—*Revelation vi, 7–8.*